Cognella Series on Career Development in Criminology and Criminal Justice

Teaching Research Methods

First Edition

Tina L. Freiburger and
Alyssa M. Sheeran

University of Wisconsin—Milwaukee

cognella® | ACADEMIC PUBLISHING

Bassim Hamadeh, CEO and Publisher
Mary Jane Peluso, Senior Specialist Acquisitions Editor
Christian Berk, Associate Production Editor
Miguel Macias, Senior Graphic Designer
Sara Schennum, Licensing Associate
Don Kesner, Interior Designer
Natalie Piccotti, Director of Marketing
Kassie Graves, Vice President of Editorial
Jamie Giganti, Director of Academic Publishing

Printed in the United States of America.

ISBN: 978-1-5165-2627-7 (pbk) / 978-1-5165-2628-4 (br)

cognella® | ACADEMIC PUBLISHING

Teaching Research Methods

BRIEF CONTENTS

DETAILED CONTENTS

Preface

Every year, new professors and instructors enter higher education in the field of criminology and criminal justice. These may be individuals who are new graduates of a Ph.D. program or retired practitioners who are starting a new career or teaching part time. No matter the stage in life, no one enters a teaching position at a college or university with all the answers. The purpose of this series is both to provide fresh teaching ideas to these professors and instructors on how to make the most of their classroom experience, as well as to provide books with career development tips and insights for those interested in an academic career.

Each of the brief teaching books is written by an expert in the field who has taught this topic for many years. The experts will provide suggestions for syllabus construction, encouraging discussion, and classroom management. Each book will provide examples of activities, discussion topics, and case studies that could be used for important topics, as well as useful documentaries, websites, etc. to use for media exploration purposes. Most important, the teaching books provide examples of tried-and-true successes in the classroom—and the failures that crashed and burned.

We hope this book and other teaching titles in this series will help both the newest academics and seasoned professionals best utilize their time in the classroom. And most important, we hope this time in the classroom will generate real enthusiasm and even excitement about the course topics for students and inspire future professionals to change the field for the better.

Sincerely,
Cathy Marcum and Jerry Westby, Editors

Author Biographies

Tina L. Freiburger is a professor and chair of the Department of Criminal Justice at the University of Wisconsin–Milwaukee. She teaches both undergraduate and graduate courses, including Analysis of Criminal Justice Research, Perspectives in Crime and the Criminal Justice System, Methods in Social Welfare Research, Crime and Criminal Justice Policy, and Juvenile Justice. Dr. Freiburger has published several journal articles on racial and gender disparities in decision-making and juvenile justice issues. She is the coauthor of *Race and Ethnic Issues in the Juvenile Justice System* and coeditor of *Women in the Criminal Justice System: Tracking the Journey of Women and Crime.* She has also published numerous peer-reviewed journal articles.

Alyssa M. Sheeran is a doctoral student and research assistant in the Department of Criminal Justice at the University of Wisconsin–Milwaukee. Her research interests focus on public perceptions of the police, juvenile justice, sentencing disparities in the criminal justice system, and individual- and neighborhood-level influences on recidivism. She holds a master's degree in criminal justice from the University of Wisconsin–Milwaukee. Sheeran has worked on projects related to juveniles' perceptions of the police, elderly prisoner misconduct, gender and racial disparities in sentencing decisions, adult drug treatment court, and veterans' court. She also teaches courses in Methods in Social Welfare Research and Crime and Criminal Justice Policy.

CHAPTER 1

Introduction

KEY CONCEPTS IN THE CHAPTER:

- Challenges in teaching criminal justice research methods
- Setting expectations for student interest
- Outline of proceeding chapters

Social science research methods can be one of the most challenging courses to teach. Often, this is not due to a lack of passion for the material on the part of the instructor. To the contrary, most instructors continued school beyond their undergraduate degrees because they were interested in being consumers and producers of research. Many of our students, however, do not share this passion.

Imagine an undergraduate student who has dreamed of being a police officer since she was young. Her best friend's goals changed multiple times growing up. He wanted to be a teacher in kindergarten, an astronaut in fourth grade, a veterinarian in eighth grade, and finally decided on accounting in college. Her goal, however, never wavered. She always knew she would be a police officer. Knowing that many departments prefer a college degree, she enrolled at the university right after high school with a major in criminal justice; she is eager to complete her degree and get on the street. Being a police officer is the ideal career for her. She likes to be active, preferring not to have to sit for long periods, and she enjoys being around other people. As a police officer, she would be outside instead of stuck at a desk, and she would be among other officers and members of the community. During her criminal justice courses, she has enjoyed learning why people might commit crime, the organization of police departments, community and police interactions, the courts and correctional systems that process those who are arrested, and the entities that serve victims of crimes. Now she has to take research methods. She is expected to learn abstract concepts and read about research studies that took place in other cities and in other states. Readings require her to sift through statistics that she does not understand and read findings from methodologies that are foreign to her. Lectures involve her instructor talking about things like concepts, operational definitions, sampling, and creating surveys. None of these seem to have any relationship to policing. This course seems too far removed from what she wants to do when she graduates. The instructor is nice and enthusiastic but the lectures seem to go on forever.

Our hypothetical student is not atypical of our real students. After graduation, many plan to pursue careers in the field of criminal justice. It is difficult for them to see how research methods will be of any benefit to them. Most of us try to convince them that research methods will help them in their careers, which is often true. Even if they come to understand that this is a possibility, it does not make discussions of validity and reliability or experimental and quasi-experimental designs any more interesting.

While teaching research methods, it is not unusual to have a small number of students who enter the course with an interest in research methods or develop an interest over the term of the course. For most of our students, like our hypothetical student, however, research methods will never be one of their favorite courses. This text is devoted to helping instructors improve the class experience for both types of students. Students do not have to develop a passion for research methods to understand it or to even have a relatively pleasant experience in the course. Throughout the following chapters, we provide examples, ideas, tips, and activities that can be used when teaching research methods to help engage students and provide them with the opportunity to apply research methods to the things they are interested in, with the goal of getting students better engaged in the course and to enhance student learning.

Chapter Outline

The importance of developing course learning objectives is the topic of Chapter 2. A short discussion is provided explaining how to develop effective course objectives. As part of the development of learning objectives, Bloom's taxonomy is presented and applied to the development of learning objectives for a criminal justice research methods course. Using learning objectives as part of the course assessments both during and after a course also is discussed. Lastly, the importance of including student self-assessments to gauge students' perceptions of their mastery of the learning objectives is included.

Class format is the topic of Chapter 3. The chapter discusses breaking lectures into small segments as a more effective way to teach research methods concepts and enhance student learning. Next, the application of concepts such as activating prior knowledge and deliberate practice are presented. Finally, the importance of reinforcing the application of concepts through repetition is further addressed.

Engaging students through independent and small group work is the subject of Chapter 4. Different styles of teaching are offered that can enhance the learning process for both instructors and students. From these, various types of active learning strategies, such as individual and group learning, clarification pause, muddiest/clearest, and minute paper are explained. The use of study groups and group projects also are examined. Ripe with examples, this chapter provides instructors with specific ideas, tips, and assignments they can incorporate into their research methods courses.

Chapter 5 offers insight for incorporating peer-reviewed articles into research methods courses. Oftentimes, students' first exposure to peer-reviewed articles will be in their undergraduate research methods courses. They will likely be required to utilize peer-reviewed articles for such things as course readings, assignments, quizzes, and class activities. This chapter provides tips to choosing appropriate peer-reviewed articles, as well as teaching students to pick their own peer-reviewed articles. Suggestions for helping students read and understand peer-reviewed articles also are provided, along with an exercise that can be used to help guide students as they complete these readings. Lastly, the chapter provides a discussion on assessing students' understanding of the content of peer-reviewed articles.

Chapter 6 focuses on teaching research methods students American Psychological Association (APA) style. The benefits of teaching students APA are discussed. Such benefits include training students to produce high-quality written documents, to teach students to consider the source from which they receive information, and to prevent plagiarism. Best practices in teaching APA also are discussed, including the advantages and disadvantages of using class instruction time to teach these techniques versus requiring students to master these techniques independently outside of class. The chapter provides several examples of assignments and activities for APA instruction. Lastly, grading tips specific to assessing mastery of APA are presented.

The last chapter in the text, Chapter 7, provides a dialogue on assessing student learning. The importance of testing is discussed, offering insight into the benefits that quizzes and examinations offer to student learning. In addition, various forms of assessment are presented that can be incorporated into an instructor's course curriculum. Examples of these include in-class quizzes, online quizzes, traditional assessments, and performance-based assessments. Finally, information is presented related to utilizing textbook or publisher-supplied assessment tools.

CHAPTER 2

Developing Course Objectives

KEY CONCEPTS IN THE CHAPTER:

- Best practices in developing course objectives
- Developing course learning objectives
- Determining appropriate dimensions for learning objectives
- Assessment of student learning objectives

When developing your research methods class, it is important to think about what you want your students to learn in your course. Assuming that most of your students will not go on to careers in research after completing their undergraduate studies, it is important to consider where research methods fits into their general criminal justice education. For instructors in most programs, students will be better served by becoming informed consumers of research than they will be as producers of research. For students who go on to work in the criminal justice field, being informed consumers will allow them to incorporate best practices into their decision-making, assess findings of evaluations conducted on the programs with which they work, determine how to match the population they serve with the best programing possible, and determine which evaluators will best serve their needs when contracting such services. For students who go on to graduate school, they will learn the first step of producing good research, as it is imperative to first understand research before conducting one's own. Once in graduate school, these students will be exposed to courses focused on learning specific skills in conducting research.

Once you determine what you want students to learn in the course, the next step is to develop learning objectives for the course and communicate them to your students. This chapter will first provide a general discussion regarding the methods to which learning objectives are developed, followed by a specific discussion of how these approaches apply to learning objectives in research methods. Next, the chapter will explain how these learning objectives can be used to assess the course so instructors know whether students are meeting the identified objectives.

Creating Learning Objectives

Learning objectives are statements that are used to communicate to students what they can expect to learn in a class. They should be specific statements regarding the knowledge, skills, and competencies that instructors expect students to acquire in a course (Suskie, 2004). Learning outcomes must possess three characteristics. According to Suskie (2004), they must specify an action that is observable, that is measurable, and that is performed by the students. In addition, learning outcomes should be statements of what students will *be able to* do and not just what they *will* do. Read through the examples below.

Students will learn about basic research designs

Students will understand basic research designs

Students will be able to identify the strengths and weakness of basic research designs

Which is the best learning objective? Notice the similarities and differences between the three learning objective statements above. All three focus on the student and contain action verbs. The first, however, states what students will do during the course. The second and third objectives focus on what students will be able to do once they complete the course. Because we want to focus on the knowledge, skills, and competencies students will acquire in a course, the second and third are better learning objectives than the first. Now if we compare the second and the third, we see that the second objective states that students will *understand* basic research designs whereas the third objective is more specific by defining what we mean by *understand*. In that objective, *understand* is defined as being able to identify strengths and weaknesses. If we want to assess our students' competency toward our learning objective, it would be easier to observe and measure students' abilities to identify strengths and weakness of basic research designs through oral or written testing than it would be to assess students' understanding. Therefore, the third statement is the best learning objective.

When developing learning objectives instructors must consider the grade level of their courses. Programs commonly list a research methods course as a junior- or senior-level course given the difficulty of the content. If the course is appropriately organized in the curriculum at this level, instructors will want to include learning objectives that tap into the higher dimensions of learning (but possibly not the highest). Determining levels of learning and communicating them to students also can improve student performance and the ability of advisors to recommend appropriate courses to students (Gerdes & Crews, 2010). Bloom's taxonomy can be beneficial in determining which dimensions are most appropriate for your course.

Bloom's Taxonomy

Bloom's taxonomy was developed to create a framework to guide the construction of learning outcomes. This taxonomy allows instructors to consider the grade level of the course as well as the level of difficulty of the course content. It includes six domains: Knowledge, Comprehension, Application, Analysis, Synthesis, and Evaluation. The domains range from simple to complex, with mastery of the simpler domains required prior to mastery of the next, more complex domains (Bloom, Engelhart, Furst, Hill, & Krathwohl, 1956). For example, students should master familiarity with a term and its definition before being expected to apply that term to an example.

With the exception of Application, the domains are further divided into subcategories. Knowledge is composed of the knowledge of terminology and specific facts; knowledge of the means of dealing with specific conventions, trends, classifications, criteria, and methodologies; and knowledge of general ideas and theories (Bloom et al., 1956). In research methods, this could involve the memorization of definitions and important statistics, the ability to remember the names of specific research designs, and the ability to list criteria to evaluate a research design. The second domain, Comprehension, is broken down into translation, interpretation, and extrapolation (Bloom et al., 1956). In a research methods course, Comprehension might include students' abilities to provide examples of relationships between dependent and independent variables. Analysis includes the analysis of elements, relationships, and organizational principles (Bloom et al., 1956). A task in research methods that might involve Analysis is the ability to construct good survey questions. Synthesis involves the production of unique communication, the production of a plan, and an understanding of abstract concepts (Bloom et al., 1956). For research methods, this might include students' abilities to determine which research design is most appropriate in which research scenario. Lastly, Evaluation includes the critique and judgment of internal and external evidence (Bloom et al., 1956). In research methods, this might involve students understanding of which type of knowledge can be produced by each research design and to what extent that knowledge can be generalized given each design.

Bloom's taxonomy was later revised by Anderson and Krathwohl (2001). Their revision adds a fourth category to the Knowledge domain, which they termed Metacognitive Knowledge. This category involves students' understanding of their own cognition and the ability to adapt the way they think due to this awareness. Anderson and Krathwohl (2001) also changed the name of this domain from Knowledge to Remember and reworded the terminology in the other three Knowledge categories. They renamed the Comprehension domain to Understand. Application, Analysis, and Evaluation were simply changed to their verb forms. Therefore, they became Apply, Analyze, and Evaluate. Synthesize was changed to Create, and the order of Evaluate and Create was switched so Create became the highest-ordered domain (Krathwohl, 2002).

Learning Objectives for Criminal Justice Research Methods

Although an undergraduate research methods course will want to include learning objectives in the higher domains, it should also include Knowledge/ Remember learning objectives, as many of the concepts will be new to the students. Students in criminal justice spend a lot of time in other courses learning the plethora of terminology used within the criminal justice system. In research methods, however, their exposure to research terminology will likely be limited to a few terms they learned in a statistics or natural science course. Therefore, they must become familiar with an entirely new field of terminology. It is important that students are able to correctly use this terminology and know the meaning of these terms when they read and hear them.

As discussed earlier, learning objectives should focus on what students will be able to do at the conclusion of the course. Therefore, each learning objective should contain an action verb(s). Some action verbs fit better in some domains than others. Table 2.1 contains some action verbs that are often associated with each domain (Kansas State University, 2003).

Table 2.1 Action Words for Bloom's Six Domains

Knowledge/ Remember	Comprehension/ Understand	Application/ Apply	Analysis/ Analyze	Evaluation/ Evaluate	Synthesis/ Create
Remember	Explain	Apply	Analyze	Assess	Combine
Memorize	Rephrase	Demonstrate	Combine	Compare	Create
Read	Discuss	Interpolate	Separate	Contrast	Compile
Recall	Distinguish	Examine	Design	Determine	Plan
Repeat	Outline	Solve	Differentiate	Judge	Derive
Recite	Provide examples	Translate	Infer	Justify	Order
State		Classify	Select	Rank	Reconstruct
Write		Discover	Utilize	Rate	Reorder
Name					Rewrite
Identify					Summarize
List					
Match					
Quote					

When constructing outcomes for classes, it is better to focus on more general concepts, skills, and competencies, keeping the number of objectives to fewer than 10. Again, it is important to remember to use action verbs in the student learning outcomes. Such learning objectives for a research methods course might include statements like:

> *Identify* and *define* basic research methods terms and concepts
>
> *Outline* the scientific method that is used by criminal justice researchers
>
> *Apply* the principles of research methods to practical problems in the criminal justice field
>
> *Compare* and *contrast* the different types of research designs and measures of crime
>
> *Analyze* the methodologies and data sources used in criminal justice research
>
> *Compare* the utility of research findings given the definition of variables, research design, data source used, and sample/population studied

Notice how each of these objectives contain action verbs, tap into various learning domains, and are focused on what students will be able to do once they complete the course. Each one also is general enough to encompass many individual concepts but uses verbs that are specific enough to be observed and measured through assessment.

Assessment of Learning Objectives

Once learning objectives are developed, instructors will want to create an assessment to determine how well students are mastering the knowledge expected. An assessment should include the collection of data on student knowledge, skills, and competencies. These data should then be reviewed and used to develop an understanding of students' mastery of the identified outcomes. If students are not acquiring the knowledge, skills, and competencies specified in the outcomes, modifications should be made to the course content instruction as appropriate. It also might be necessary to include additional opportunities for students to learn. This could be in the form of additional assignments, the employment of multiple methods of teaching the same material (e.g., providing a visual, written, and oral explanation of concepts), or the addition of in-class and out-of-class applications. Further assessments should continue to determine which methods are most effective at reaching the outcomes (Palomba & Banta, 2014).

When we think of assessments, it is easy to envision a one-time "test" to determine student mastery of outcomes. This could take place after the course and be used to inform future instruction. Although this is less labor-intensive than continuous assessment, the disadvantage of limiting assessment to a one-time process is that it does not provide the opportunity to address gaps in student knowledge before the course ends. Therefore, while future students can benefit from end-of-the-term assessments, current students do not. If instructors, instead, build assessments into the course regularly, they can identify areas of student confusion and provide additional opportunities to teach students those areas.

It is also easy to think of ongoing assessments of course knowledge as periodic testing. Instructors might utilize a midterm and a final, or more frequent tests (e.g., three exams every 5 weeks) throughout the semester that are used to evaluate students' grades. While an informative part of assessment, testing is limited because it is more difficult to go back and reteach a concept after students have been tested on it. If the concept will not appear on another exam or assignment, many students will likely focus little attention on it as a way to manage their time to focus on concepts that will appear on future exams and assignments. Going back to prior concepts also can be difficult for instructors who are trying to cover a large amount of information over the semester. Having to revisit concepts can limit the time they have available to teach new material. In addition, if students are not understanding certain concepts their grades will be negatively affected before they are afforded additional opportunities to enhance their learning.

It is best, therefore, for instructors to provide low-stakes (either not graded or worth only a few points) assessments of student learning throughout course instruction. Instructors could do this through course discussion, in-class activities, group activities, etc. Many examples of these are provided in other chapters of this text (e.g., see muddiest/clearest point exercise in Chapter 4). Utilizing these techniques can alert an instructor of the need to provide additional examples, add additional lecture time for the concept, increase group or individual assignments, offer more quizzes, or include more practice activities on concepts that students are finding problematic. If the majority of the class is having difficulty, the instructor can use class time to do this. If fewer than half of the class is having difficulty, the instructor can hold an additional study session or simply provide additional examples and practice activities to the students having difficulties. Students must then have the opportunity to go over these activities with the instructor or teaching assistant and receive feedback to determine whether they need further help.

In addition to these more informal assessments, programs also should consider larger assessments to gauge student learning. These might be pretests and posttests at the beginning and end of the term or performance on specific assignments, papers, or exam/quiz questions. It is best if these assessments are uniform across all sections of the course and all instructors who teach the course. These assessments can be course specific or can encompass mastery of the entire program (e.g., when students enter the major and again when they graduate). These assessments also can take the form of final papers or projects such as a senior synthesis or capstone project. If course specific, instructors might consider developing more specific learning outcomes to more clearly communicate to instructors what specific knowledge, skills, and competencies students should possess at the end of the course.

SPECIFIC LEARNING OBJECTIVES

Learning Objective for Knowledge/Remember

- Students will be able to *identify* key research methods terms and their definitions

Learning Objectives for Comprehension/Understand

- Students will be able to *discuss* the importance of reliable and valid measurement
- Students will be able *distinguish* between independent and dependent variables

Learning Objective for Application/Apply

- Students will be able to *apply* the appropriate sampling method to a given population and research question

Learning Objective for Analyze

- Students will be able to *design* a survey question that meets all recommended guidelines

Learning Objectives for Evaluate

- Students will be able to *assess* the reliability and validity of a measurement
- Students will be able to *assess* the quality of the operational definition of a variable

Learning Objectives for Create

- Students will be able to *create* conceptual definitions, operational definitions, and measurements for concepts
- Students will be able to *create* a research study to assess a hypothesis

Each learning objective presented here begins with "Students will"; however, when presenting learning objectives, instructors often leave these words off.

Reading through the learning objectives in the Specific Learning Objectives example, notice how they become increasingly difficult as you pass from one to the next. It is important for each instructor to consider which aspects of the content are most important to them and their program when writing the learning objectives, as some of these examples might not be the learning objectives they feel are important for students to master in their courses. Although, there should be some uniformity across programs, it is expected that there will be some variation as the goals of different programs and the students to whom they serve are somewhat different. For many undergraduate programs, it will likely make more sense to identify learning objectives in the first three or four learning domains. Most learning objectives in the latter domains will fit better into a graduate-level research methods course. These outcomes can be useful in creating assessments of courses to determine whether students are acquiring the specific knowledge intended.

Student Experience

In addition to an objective assessment of student learning, instructors also should consider incorporating student feedback regarding how well students feel they have mastered the identified learning objectives. This can be done through a self-survey administered to students. Such surveys can contain questions asking students to rate on a Likert scale their ability to complete the stated course learning objectives. For example, students could be asked whether they strongly disagree, disagree, agree, or strongly agree that they are able to apply the principles of research methods to practical problems in the criminal justice field.

Questions also can be included for more specific learning outcomes, such as asking students whether they strongly disagree, disagree, agree, or strongly agree that they are able to discuss the importance of reliable and valid measurement. This can be made even more specific by asking about specific assignments or activities. For example, a question might ask whether students strongly disagree, disagree, agree, or strongly agree that the Independent Work for Learning Variables worksheet (see example in Chapter 4) improved their ability to distinguish between independent and dependent variables. These types of questions can help instructors understand which teaching methodologies are contributing most to enhancing student learning. The most effective methods can then be shared among instructors to create a course template for all instructors across all sections of the course. Results of these student self-assessments also can be compared to the results of the other assessments to determine if any gaps exist.

Summary

Prior to teaching a research methods course, instructors should take some time to think about what they want their students to get out of their class. These expectations should then be used to craft student learning objectives for the course that are shared with students. Student learning objectives should be statements that focus on what students will acquire from the course and contain action verbs that can be observed and measured. These learning objectives serve an important purpose, as they allow instructors to assess students' mastery of the course material. These assessments should be ongoing to improve student learning throughout the course as well as at the conclusion of the course to improve future courses.

References

Anderson, L. W. (Ed.), Krathwohl, D. R. (Ed.), Airasian, P. W., Cruikshank, K. A., Mayer, R. E., Pintrich, P. R., Raths, J., & Wittrock, M. C. (2001). *A taxonomy for learning, teaching, and assessing: A revision of Bloom's taxonomy of educational objectives* (Complete edition). New York, NY: Longman.

Bloom, B. S. (Ed.), Engelhart, M. D., Furst, E. J., Hill, W. H., & Krathwohl, D. R. (1956). *Taxonomy of educational objectives: The classification of educational goals. Handbook 1: Cognitive domain.* New York, NY: Addison Wesley Longman.

Gerdes, J. H., & Crews, T. B. (2010). Developing course profiles to match course characteristics with student learning styles. *NACADA Journal, 30*(1), 23–33.

Kansas State University. (2003). How to write student learning outcomes: Action verb list—suggested verbs to use in each level of thinking skills. Retrieved April 12, 2018, from https://www.k-state.edu/assessment/toolkit/outcomes/action.html

Krathwohl, D. R. (2002). A revision of Bloom's taxonomy: An overview. *Theory into Practice, 41*(4), 212–218.

Palombo, C. A., & Banta, T. W. (2014). *Assessment essentials: Planning, implementing, and improving assessments in higher education.* San Francisco, CA: Jossey-Bass.

Suskie, L. (2004). *Assessing student learning: A common sense guide.* Bolton, MA: Anker.

Credits

Table 2.1: Dr. Cia Verschelden, https://www.k-state.edu/assessment/toolkit/outcomes/action.html. Copyright © 2003 by Kansas State University.

CHAPTER 3

Class Format

KEY CONCEPTS IN THE CHAPTER:

- Breaking lectures into small segments
- Practicing the application of concepts
- Reinforcing the application of concepts through repetition

As you prepare the syllabus for your upcoming course in research methods, you may find yourself wondering what content to include, how many assignments and exams will be necessary, what is the best way to present the material, etc. Do you engage in a traditional lecture method, while including several assignments and exams to test students' retention of the information? Or do you utilize a more interactive approach, incorporating active learning techniques that allow students additional practice in applying concepts to real-life situations? Determining how you will format your course can influence the level of learning in which students engage. Although most college classrooms still utilize the traditional lecture to present information, this may not be the most effective method of class presentation for courses in research methods, considering that most of the course learning objectives include the application of information and the development of problem-solving skills. This chapter discusses an alternative class format that will allow students the opportunity to remain engaged, practice the application of concepts, and develop long-term retention of information related to research methods.

Breaking Lectures into Small Segments

The traditional lecture method remains the most prevalent form of content delivery in college classrooms today. Not only do lectures require less preparation for the instructor, but they are the most cost-efficient way to teach substantive information to a large number of students at once (Chambers & Blake, 2007; Frederick, 1986; Hake, 1998). A well-delivered lecture can be compelling and engaging, where the instructor is able to present, explain, and clarify new information; however, it is often recognized that few lectures actually achieve this ideal (Frederick, 1986). Research has repeatedly shown that lectures are an ineffective method for students to retain information and engage in deep learning (Mazur, 1997; McLeish, 1968; Powell, 2003). Moreover, interviews with both instructors and students have revealed numerous limitations of the lecture method. Faculty members have shared that attendance tends to be significantly lower in lectures, engagement within the class is missing, and there is a lack of preparedness from students (Fink, 2013; Walker, Cotner, Baepler, & Decker, 2008). From the perspectives of students, interviews have discovered that students have a hard time staying focused during lectures and find them monotonous. Students also stated that it is difficult for them to see the significance of what they are learning (Fink, 2013). These opinions seem logical considering that a great deal of research has determined that students' attention spans are only 15 to 20 minutes long (Bligh, 2000; Burns, 1985; Hartley & Davies, 1978; Horowitz, 1988; Stuart & Rutherford, 1978; Wankat, 2002). As such, these criticisms lead many practitioners to believe that a new form of teaching is needed to ensure that students are benefiting the most from their learning experience.

Many instructors have begun incorporating active learning methods into the classroom that involve greater interaction between the students and the instructor. This method of content delivery integrates exercises into the classroom, rather than having students listen passively to an instructor's lecture (Faust & Paulson, 1998). Research finds that students learn best when they are engaged in an instructor-guided environment that develops the skills necessary for retaining information (Toto & Booth, 2008). These efforts to improve courses through active learning have been routinely noted in prior research, demonstrating positive results compared to the traditional lecture (Freeman et al., 2007; Knight & Wood, 2005; McClanahan & McClanahan, 2002). For example, a study conducted by Walker and colleagues (2008) tested a traditional lecture versus active learning techniques and determined that students' final grades were significantly better in the active section, with students at the bottom end of the grade distribution benefiting the most from active learning. Consequently, this method is best utilized with courses whose goals involve the application of information and the development of problem-solving skills, making them especially useful for classes related to research methods. Several varieties of the active learning method are discussed in Chapter 4, and it is crucial for instructors to determine which style and exercises will be most appropriate for their class.

As with any form of class presentation, no method is without limitations. Critics of the active learning method have noted that incorporating these techniques can make it difficult for the instructor to cover all class material during designated class meetings (Pasley, Weiss, Shimkus, & Smith, 2004; Walker et al., 2008). Instructors who teach research methods may find this shortcoming all too familiar, considering there is a vast amount of information to cover that most students find difficult to grasp. While this may be true, this limitation can be overcome in several ways. First, the instructor should decide which course topics require a greater degree of application and understanding, and then integrate either more or fewer active learning exercises into the class accordingly. For example, material related to criteria for causality or validity may require additional active learning exercises than field research or qualitative interviewing. Planning this way can preserve more time in certain class meetings to present additional material. Second, instructors can assign material outside of class for students to learn; however, this should be saved for content that is less intensive for students to understand. This can be in the form of an assignment or online quiz (graded or not) to ensure that students have reviewed and understood the material. Although one might assume that students would not follow through with this work, Walker and colleagues (2008) found that students did not mind being held responsible for material outside of class, as long as they were made aware of what was expected of them and where to find the material.

Other criticisms of active learning include resistance from the students. Traditional lectures are the most prevalent form of class presentation, and therefore students may resist any other teaching style that is presented to them. Some students have shared that active learning techniques "simplify the lecture" and they feel they are not being taught enough material (Young, 2008). To avoid resistance, it is important for instructors to inform their students at the beginning of the course that these techniques will be utilized to help students understand more difficult concepts throughout the course. This will likely increase students' perceptions that the activities will be beneficial to their needs, especially in a course such as research methods where the material tends to be more difficult to grasp compared to that presented in other criminal justice courses (Young, 2008).

A middle ground between the popular traditional lecture and active learning techniques that satisfies both the students and the instructor is the mini-lecture. Mini-lectures allow instructors to utilize a blend of both traditional presentation and active learning exercises. These are short lectures that last 15 minutes or less and are followed by active learning exercises that allow students to practice the application of concepts (Walker et al., 2008). For example, an instructor may lecture briefly on the definition and significance of independent and dependent variables, and then have students break off into small groups to complete an exercise where they identify the variables in different hypotheses. For larger class sizes, instructors can still incorporate active learning techniques by having students work alone or in pairs. A few volunteers can then share their answers to the class at large, providing public feedback for both the rest of the class and the instructor, without taking up too much of the class period (Frederick, 1986). Professors who have utilized mini-lectures have noticed from their own experiences that the short breaks are advantageous. Students tend to concentrate better when the energy shifts back to the instructor for the next brief lecture, which helps to counter the attention span problem discussed earlier (Frederick, 1986). Additionally, blended class formats increase students' perceptions that they are learning, it makes classes feel shorter, and students seem to grasp the material better because they know how to apply the concepts rather than simply memorizing terms (Walker et al., 2008; Young, 2008).

Practicing the Application of Concepts

Again, the traditional lecture method habitually requires students to memorize a substantive amount of information, resulting in an inefficient way to promote understanding of course content. Utilizing active learning techniques into research methods courses will allow students the ability to practice the application of concepts with real-world situations. This section discusses two such approaches that can be utilized in a research methods course to help students better retain information and engage in deep learning.

Activating Prior Knowledge

Prior knowledge is a crucial variable in learning (Alexander, Kulikowich, & Schulze, 1992), and has been defined in a variety of ways throughout the literature. Jonassen and Gabrowski (1993) refer to prior knowledge as the skills and abilities that students bring to the learning process. Others have defined it simply as what one already knows about a subject (Stevens, 1980) or the knowledge that one has when entering a learning environment that is potentially relevant for securing new knowledge (Biemens, Deel, & Simons, 2001). Despite how one might define prior knowledge, what students already know about certain content is one of the strongest predictors of how well they will learn new information relative to that content (Alessi & Trollip, 1991; Christen & Murphy, 1991; Marzano, 2004). Through engaging in personal meaning and real-world situations, students must become skillful at activating prior knowledge, assimilating it with new information, and constructing new understandings. Students who lack this information will likely struggle to learn and progress through the course curriculum (Chinn & Brewer, 1993; Guzzetti, Snyder, Glass, & Gamas, 1993; Strangman, Hall, & Meyer, 2004). Therefore, instructors need to provide a learning environment that integrates stability and familiarity, and challenges students to call on prior knowledge when engaging in deep learning (Christen & Murphy, 1991).

For instructors who are teaching graduate-level methods courses, activating students' prior knowledge related to research methods will be much easier compared to instructors in undergraduate-level courses. Nonetheless, this section describes several strategies that will assist instructors in activating and developing background knowledge. First, whether at the undergraduate or graduate level, instructors must determine the level of background knowledge within the class. This can either be done at the beginning of the course or before a specific topic is presented. Most undergraduate students will not have much prior knowledge related to research methods; however, they most likely have some background knowledge in mathematics, social sciences, and even personal experiences. This can be used to bring personal meaning and connections to certain topics within the course. Instructors can have students "reflect and record" what they may already know about a concept or have students respond to specific questions that are presented by the instructor (Carr & Thompson, 1996; Christen & Murphy, 1991; Spires & Donley, 1998). Additionally, the instructor can incorporate an "anticipation guide," where true-false statements are provided to the students about important course content, allowing the instructor to analyze the quality and quantity of background knowledge (Anders & Spitler, 2007; Lent, 2012). Figure 3.1 provides an example of an anticipation guide that can be used for course content related to variables. By utilizing any of these methods, instructors can determine the level of background knowledge related to certain content and will gain a useful guide for how much time needs to be spent teaching new material.

Figure 3.1 Anticipation Guide

Anticipation Guide on Variables		
Read each statement below and circle "True" if you believe the statement is correct or "False" if you believe the statement is incorrect.		
	True/False	
1. Variables are a logical grouping of attributes.	True	False
2. The independent variable is the variable being explained/predicted.	True	False
3. Attributes are characteristics that describe some object.	True	False
4. The dependent variable causes a change in the independent variable.	True	False
5. Understanding the relationship between variables is helpful because it establishes correlation and improves guesses.	True	False

The literature on activating prior knowledge provides a variety of strategies that can be integrated into the classroom to not only assist in building background knowledge, but to help focus attention and guide students during and after the class meeting (Christen & Murphy, 1991). It is advantageous if the instructor explicitly helps students connect what they already know about a topic to what is required of them to learn (Lent, 2012). For undergraduate students, this may mean relating similar experiences outside of research methods to the course content or examples within active learning exercises. For instance, students have had some form of mathematical training prior to enrolling in a research methods course. When covering content related to simple statistics and data interpretation, it would be wise to activate their background knowledge associated with mathematics to the new course content related specifically to research methods.

Another strategy for building background knowledge is to have students answer both pre- and post-questions associated with new material. This can be a simple active learning exercise completed outside of class or briefly during the designated class meeting. Before new material is presented, students should be instructed to answer pre-questions about the new content. This will create helpful cues on what to pay attention to throughout the reading or presentation of new material (Clark, 2003; Pressley, Wood, Woloshyn, & Martin, 1992; Rowe & Rayford, 1987). Whether their answers are correct or not, learning related to these pre-questions should be enhanced (Pressley et al., 1992). The same questions can be administered once the material is presented, giving the instructor direct feedback on the understanding of the course content. Not only do these strategies aid in activating prior knowledge, but they help focus and build background knowledge that will provide a conceptual framework for future use.

PRE- AND POST-QUESTIONS ON CONCEPTS AND MEASUREMENT

Before students begin their assigned reading on concepts and measurements, have them answer several questions related to the content. Examples of questions may include:

- What is a conceptual definition?
- What is an operational definition?
- What does it mean for a measure to be exhaustive and exclusive, and why is this important?
- Describe each of the four levels of measurement (i.e., nominal, ordinal, interval, ratio).

After students have written down their answers you should collect their responses. Once students have read the material, the same set of questions should be readministered to the students. You should then collect the post-responses and compare students' answers on the pre- and post-questions. This will allow you to gauge students' understanding of concepts and measurements. Students should then receive both their pre- and post-responses, where they can reflect on how their answers may have either changed or remained stable throughout the activity.

Deliberate Practice

Although activating prior knowledge is an important component to deep learning, practicing the application of concepts more intensively will likely lead to further improvements in students' performance levels. "Deliberate practice" has been coined in the literature as the engagement in highly structured activities that are created to specifically improve performance through focused goals, direct feedback, and opportunities for repetition (Ericsson, 1996, 2002; Ericcson, Krampe, & Tesch-Romer, 1993). Students must initially learn the underlying meaning of a new concept or idea. Thus, it is essential for students to practice the application of that concept, receive feedback on their mistakes, and gradually develop the ability to internalize and avoid those errors (Anderson 1982, 1987; Fitts & Posner, 1967). As a result, students are able to develop high levels of comprehension and expert performance on a regular basis. Studies that have examined the relationship between deliberate practice and performance level have found positive correlations, where high levels of deliberate practice were associated with high levels of performance outcomes (Macnamara, Hambrick, & Oswald, 2014).

The incorporation of deliberate practice into research methods courses is especially crucial because much of the course content requires students to apply the knowledge to real-world situations. With an active learning style of presentation, exercises presented to students will allow them the opportunity to practice concepts and receive feedback on their efforts, ultimately affording them the ability to retain important information (examples of specific active learning exercises will be presented in Chapter 4).

INTEGRATING DELIBERATE PRACTICE METHODS INTO THE CLASSROOM

When introducing the three criteria for causation, you should first conduct a brief lecture on the definition and significance of this criteria, while also providing several examples to illustrate the new material. After the brief lecture, students can break into pairs to practice applying the concepts they just learned through a worksheet that lists several hypotheses. Students should be instructed to identify whether each of the three criteria for causation have been met, and *why* they believe so. They should also identify possible spurious factors that could potentially influence the relationship. Once students have completed the worksheet, you should review the correct answers with the entire class, allowing students to receive immediate feedback. The practice of this application should additionally be incorporated into assignments outside of the classroom, as well as on examinations. However, if a higher level of performance is to be expected, practice on the criteria for causation should not end after the exam. For instance, when students begin to learn about experimental and quasi-experimental designs, it would be beneficial to have them continue to identify whether the causation criteria have been met in examples related to these designs through later exercises, assignments, and even subsequent exams. By doing so, students are able to continually practice the application of concepts, as well as understand how earlier course material connects to content that is presented later on in the semester.

Reinforcing the Application of Concept Through Repetition

Over the passage of time, individuals lose the ability to recall the past, producing the gradual "forgetting curve" (Cepeda, Vul, Rohrer, Wixted, & Pashler, 2008). Our memory is affected by not only what happens during the presentation of material, but also by what happens during testing trials (i.e., assignments, exams, etc.) (Dempster, 1989). This brings to light the question of whether instruction and related learning exercises can be arranged in such a way that will be optimal for deep learning. Prior literature has investigated this inquiry, suggesting that repeated presentations that are properly spaced out are an effective way of promoting long-term memory (Cepeda et al., 2008; Kang, 2016).

Spaced Repetition

A single exposure to content will not result in students' long-term retention of material (see Chapter 7 for an additional discussion). Coined the "massed effect," we often find in lectures that course content is presented during a single session, and then students cram to memorize the material right before the exam. This form of practice does not provide the opportunity for long-term retention. Instead, memory performance is most beneficial from repeated presentations of content (Bjork, 1979; Cepeda, Pashler, Vul, Wixted, & Rohrer, 2006; Ebbinghaus, 1913; Glenberg, 1976; Logan, Castel, Haber, & Viehman, 2012; Ruch, 1928; Son & Simon, 2012). Referred to as the "spacing effect," studying information across two or more sessions that are separated in time produces a deeper learning than spending the same amount of time studying in only one session (Carpenter, Cepeda, Rohrer, Kang, & Pashler, 2012; Cepeda et al., 2006; Dunlosky, Rawson, March, Nathan, & Willingham, 2013; Ebbinghaus, 1913; Kang, 2016). Let us use Figure 3.2 as a demonstration. In the first depiction (massed effect), the instructor presents the content during an initial class lecture. Then, at the end of that same lecture the instructor incorporates an active learning exercise to have students review and practice the material that was just taught. Students are then tested on that information in the form of an exam some time later. Now, in the second depiction (spaced effect) students are presented the content during an initial class lecture. The following week, the instructor integrates an active learning exercise that has students review and practice the application of the content that was learned the week prior. Then, students are administered an exam some time later that will examine their level of recall on the content (Bjork, 1979; Cepeda et al., 2008, 2009). Utilizing the spaced-effect method, students are afforded the opportunity to engage with course content over an extended period of time rather than in one class session, which ultimately enhances memory and a deeper form of learning (Kang, 2016; Wahlheim, Maddox, & Jacoby, 2014).

Figure 3.2 Massed Effect versus Spaced Effect

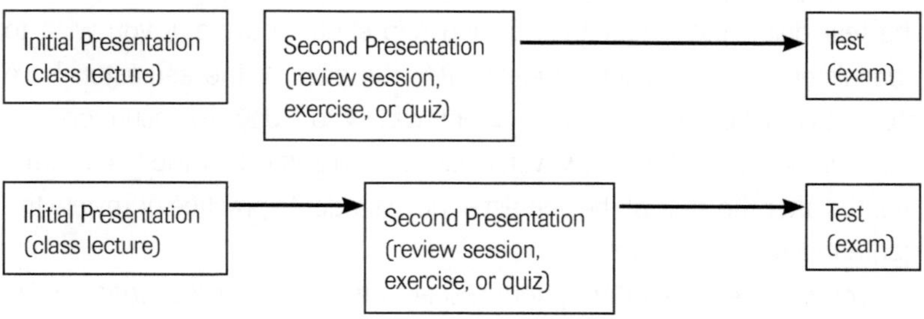

Research examining the effects of massed practice versus spaced practice continuously finds that students' performance on a delayed test is significantly improved if the practice is spaced across multiple sessions, rather than massed into a single presentation (Bahrick, 1979; Balota, Duchek, & Paullin, 1989; Bjork, 1979; Cepeda et al., 2006; Dempster, 1987, 1989; Donovan & Radosevich, 1999; Lee & Genovese, 1988). In fact, Bjork (1979) determined that individuals' level of recall following spaced presentations was more than twice the level of recall following massed presentations. Therefore, utilizing deliberate practice techniques through repetition will provide students with the greatest likelihood of developing long-term memory.

It is clear that spacing information and practice over time results in enhanced learning, however the question that still remains for instructors is: What is the optimal spacing gap? Known as the "lag effect" throughout the literature, it appears that different spacing gaps result in different degrees of learning for students. It would seem logical that longer spacing gaps would promote better retention (Glenberg, 1976; Hintzman, 1969, 1974; Kahana & Howard, 2005; Melton, 1970); however, if the gaps are too long it is possible that students may forget what they initially learned (Cepeda et al., 2006, 2009; Donovan & Radosevich, 1999; Glenberg 1976; Verkoeijen, Rikers, & Özsoy, 2008). What is important for instructors to understand is that there is no one-size-fits-all in terms of the optimal spacing gap. Instead, instructors must consider the length of their course, and when the information will be tested in the future to determine which intervals will promote the best learning environment for their students (Cepeda et al., 2008). For example, Cepeda and colleagues (2008) conducted a study to determine which spacing gap would produce the highest level of recall on a final test. Utilizing a final test that was administered after a delay of 7, 35, and 70 days, compared with a zero-day delay, the authors determined the optimal spacing gaps to be 1, 11, and 21 days. Consequently, the longer the test delay, the longer the spacing gap should be. So, if you wish to administer the first exam 1 month after the start of the semester, have students practice or review the content every 4 to 5 days to ensure optimal recall of the information. However, if you wish to administer the first exam 2 months after the start of the semester, have students practice or review the content every 8 to 9 days.

Content presented throughout research methods courses tends to be information that is more difficult for students to grasp onto and apply accurately. It is critical that students understand the basics of research methods before moving into content that is more complex. Therefore, students must repeatedly practice the material throughout the entire course. Instructors in a research methods course can easily incorporate deliberate practice with spaced repetitions into their class format through several simple strategies. Including a brief review of the previous class session at the beginning of each class period will allow students additional exposure and practice to the content (Carpenter et al., 2012; Son & Simon, 2012). This can either be in the form of a few questions posted on a PowerPoint slide, a brief exercise, or an in-class quiz that requires students to apply the concepts to various examples (see Chapter 7 for greater detail on in-class quizzing). Additionally, hosting a review session (either during or outside of class) before each exam will aid students in recalling and practicing important content.

REVIEWING AND PRACTICING EARLIER CONTENT

During the previous class meeting, students were taught the various topics appropriate to field research. At the next class meeting, students are instructed to participate in a brief exercise that requires them to design a field study that will properly investigate a given research question. The exercise can be completed individually or in small groups, and students should be given 10 to 15 minutes to complete the exercise. This exercise calls for students to recall information that was previously learned and apply that information to real-life situations:

> "As a researcher, you are interested in studying the experiences and perspectives of individuals who are currently homeless. Design a field study that will allow you to investigate this topic. Be sure to include all relevant details in your study design."

Through this exercise, students will develop strategies on gaining access to the subjects, sampling, their level of participation as a researcher, which topic areas or questions to explore, data collection, etc. Students can either share their answers with the entire class or submit their responses and receive written feedback from the instructor.

Another strategy to integrate spaced practice into the course is to utilize homework assignments or online quizzes (see Chapter 7 for greater detail on online quizzing) to re-expose students to important content that has previously been taught (Carpenter et al., 2012; Son & Simon, 2012). This strategy is especially useful when class time is limited and instructors find it difficult to fit review sessions into the class meetings. It is essential though that instructors provide feedback to the assignments so that students can learn from any mistakes that are made.

UTILIZING HOMEWORK FOR SPACED PRACTICE

Using the previous example, students have engaged in reviewing and practicing topics related to field research through the use of in-class exercises and review sessions. To re-expose them to the same content, give students a homework assignment where they must read and answer questions from a peer-reviewed article that conducted a field study. This assignment should be dispersed after the in-class exercise but before the exam review session so students have the opportunity to repeatedly practice the application of content at spaced intervals.

Finally, administering *cumulative* exams or quizzes will give students the chance to continually practice the application of concepts that are learned throughout the course. Yet, cumulative tests are often rare in universities, as Delaney and colleagues (2010) found that college professors tend to teach without repetition by giving three to four noncumulative exams throughout their courses. Incorporating cumulative tests into research methods courses may be easier than expected though, because much of the content in research methods courses already flows in a cumulative manner. For instance, fundamental concepts such as independent and dependent variables need to be understood in order to move onto subsequent content, such as how to construct an experimental design. To ensure that these concepts remain enforced, instructors can simply include a few additional questions into subsequent exams that will touch on previous material.

INCORPORATING CUMULATIVE MATERIAL

Content presented, practiced, and tested on the first exam could potentially include students' knowledge of variables, attributes, hypotheses, criteria for causation, units of analysis, etc. Following the first exam, students might begin to learn about experimental and quasi-experimental designs. To reinforce the application of previous concepts, subsequent exercises, quizzes, and exams can be constructed over spaced intervals so that students must practice current material, as well as material learned earlier in the course. If the second exam occurs 1 month after the first exam was administered, incorporate exercises, reviews, or quizzes every 4 to 5 days that will cover both new and previous material. For example, students are asked to complete an exercise where they must design an experimental study from a given hypothesis. To do so, they must first identify the independent and dependent variables, as well as the unit of analysis. After designing their experiment, they must then explain whether the criteria for causation has been met. As a result, students are engaging in repeated, spaced practice that will provide them the opportunity to enhance long-term memory.

Summary

Courses in research methods involve goals related to proficient application of information and the development of problem-solving skills. Knowing that the content provided in these courses is generally more difficult for students to grasp, alternative actions need to be implemented into the class format to ensure that students are successful at learning content in a manner for promoting long-term retention. Teaching methods such as the traditional lecture that are popular within college classrooms may not be the most appropriate for courses in research methods. We have found that an active learning style of teaching will permit the introduction of various exercises into the classroom that will help engage students in the learning process. The strategies presented in this chapter offer suggestions for instructors to integrate both practice and reinforcement of the application of concepts. It is up to the instructor to decide which strategies will be most beneficial to their classroom and their own teaching style.

References

Alessi, S. M., & Trollip, S. R. (1991). *Computer-based instruction. Methods and development* (2nd ed.). Englewood Cliffs, NJ: Prentice Hall.

Alexander, P. A., Kulikowich, J. A., & Schulze, S. K. (1992). *How subject-matter knowledge affects recall and interest.* Paper presented at the XXV International Congress of Psychology, Brussels, July.

Anders, P. L., & Spitler, E. (2007). Reinventing comprehension instruction for adolescents. In J. Lewis & G. Moorman (Eds.), *Adolescent literacy instruction: Policies and promising practices* (pp. 167–191). Newark, DE: International Reading Association.

Anderson, J. R. (1982). Acquisition of cognitive skill. *Psychological Review, 89,* 369–406.

Anderson, J. R. (1987). Skill acquisition: Compilation of weak-method problem situations. *Psychological Review, 94*(2), 192–210.

Bahrick, H. P. (1979). Maintenance of knowledge: Questions about memory we forget to ask. *Journal of Experimental Psychology: General, 108,* 296–308.

Balota, D. A., Duchek, J. M., & Paullin, R. (1989). Age-related differences in the impact of spacing, lag, and retention interval. *Psychology and Aging, 4,* 3–9.

Biemans, H. J., Deel, O. R., & Simmons, P. R. J. (2001). Differences between successful and less successful students while working with the CONTACT-2 strategy. *Learning and Instruction, 11*(4–5), 265–282.

Bjork, R. A. (1979). Information-processing analysis of college teaching. *Educational Psychologist, 14,* 15–23.

Bligh, D. A. (2000). *What's the use of lectures?* San Francisco, CA: Jossey-Bass.

Burns, R. A. (1985). *Information impact and factors affecting recall.* Presented at Annual National Conference on Teaching Excellence and Conference of Administrators, Austin, TX.

Carpenter, S. K., Cepeda, N. J., Rohrer, D., Kang, S. H. K., & Pashler, H. (2012). Using spacing to enhance diverse forms of learning: Review of recent research and implications for instruction. *Educational Psychology Review, 24,* 369–378.

Carr, S. C., & Thompson, B. (1996). The effects of prior knowledge and schema activation strategies on the inferential reading comprehension of children with and without learning disabilities. *Learning Disability Quarterly, 19,* 48–61.

Cepeda, N. J., Coburn, N., Rohrer, D., Wixted, J. T., Mozer, M. C., & Pashler, H. (2009). Optimizing distributed practice: Theoretical analysis and practical implications. *Experimental Psychology, 56,* 236–246.

Cepeda, N. J., Pashler, H., Vul, E., Wixted, J. T., & Rohrer, D. (2006). Distributed practice in verbal recall tasks: A review and quantitative synthesis. *Psychological Bulletin, 132,* 354–380.

Cepeda, N. J., Vul, E., Rohrer, D., Wixted, J. T., & Pashler, H. (2008). Spacing effects in learning: A temporal ridgeline of optimal retention. *Psychological Science, 19,* 1095–1102.

Chambers, K. A., & Blake, B. (2007). Enhancing student performance in first-semester general chemistry using active feedback through the World Wide Web. *Journal of Chemical Education, 84,* 1130–1135.

Chinn, C. A., & Brewer, W. F. (1993). The role of anomalous data in knowledge acquisition: A theoretical framework and implications for science instruction. *Review of Educational Research, 63,* 1–49.

Christen, W. L., & Murphy, T. J. (1991). *Increasing comprehension by activating prior knowledge: ERIC digest.* Bloomington, IN: ERIC Clearinghouse on Reading and Communication Skills.

Clark, R. C. (2003). *Building expertise: Cognitive methods for training and performance improvement* (2nd ed.). Washington, DC: International Society of Performance Improvement.

Delaney, P. F., Verkoeijen, P. P. J. L., & Spirgel, A. (2010). Spacing and testing effects: A deeply critical, lengthy, and at times discursive review of the literature. In B. H. Ross (Ed.), *Psychology of learning and motivation: Advances in research and theory* (Vol. 53, pp. 63–147). New York, NY: Elsevier.

Dempster, F. N. (1987). Time and the production of classroom learning: Discerning implications from basic research. *Educational Psychologist, 22,* 1–21.

Dempster, F. N. (1989). Spacing effects and their implications for theory and practice. *Educational Psychology Review, 1,* 309–330.

Donovan, J. J., & Radosevich, D. J. (1999). A meta-analytic review of the distribution of practice effect: Now you see it, now you don't. *Journal of Applied Psychology, 84,* 795–805.

Dunlosky, J., Rawson, K. A., Marsh, E. J., Nathan, M. J., & Willingham, D. T. (2013). Improving students' learning with effective learning techniques: Promising directions from cognitive and educational psychology. *Psychological Science in the Public Interest, 14,* 4–58.

Ebbinghaus, H. (1913). *Memory. A contribution to experimental psychology.* New York, NY: Teachers College, Columbia University.

Ericsson, K. A. (1996). The acquisition of expert performance: An introduction to some of the issues. In K. A. Ericsson (Ed.), *The road to excellence: The acquisition of expert performance in the arts and sciences, sports, and games* (pp. 1–50). Mahwah, NJ: Erlbaum.

Ericsson, K. A. (2002). Attaining excellence through deliberate practice: Insights from the study of expert performance. In M. Ferrari (Ed.), *The pursuit of excellence in education* (pp. 21–55). Hillsdale, NJ: Erlbaum.

Ericsson, K. A., Krampe, R. T., & Tesch-Romer, C. (1993). The role of deliberate practice in the acquisition of expert performance. *Psychological Review, 100,* 363–406.

Faust, J. L., & Paulson, D. R. (1998). Active learning in the college classroom. *Journal on Excellence in College Teaching, 9*(2), 3–24.

Fink, L. D. (2013). Creating significant learning experiences. In *Creating significant learning experiences, revised and updated: An integrated approach to designing college courses* (Chapter 1). San Francisco, CA: Jossey-Bass.

Fitts, P. M., & Posner, M. I. (1967). *Human performance.* Belmont, CA: Brooks/Cole.

Frederick, P. J. (1986). The lively lecture: 8 variations. *College Teaching, 34*(2), 43–50.

Freeman, S., O'Connor, E., Parks, J. W., Cunningham, M., Hurley, D., Haak, D., Dirks, C., & Wenderoth, M. P. (2007). Prescribed active learning increases performance in introductory biology. *CBE Life Sciences Education, 6,* 132–139.

Glenberg, A. M. (1976). Monotonic and nonmonotonic lag effects in paired-associate and recognition memory paradigms. *Journal of Verbal Learning and Verbal Behavior, 15,* 1–16.

Guzzetti, B. J., Snyder, T. E., Glass, G. V., & Gamas, W. S. (1993). Promoting conceptual change in science: A comparative meta-analysis of instructional interventions from reading education and science education. *Reading Research Quarterly, 28,* 117–155.

Hake, R. R. (1998). Interactive-engagement versus traditional methods: A six-thousand student survey of mechanics test data for introductory physics courses. *American Journal of Physics, 66,* 64–74.

Hartley, J., & Davies, I. (1978). Note taking: A critical review. *Programmed learning and Educational Technology, 15,* 207–224.

Hintzman, D. L. (1969). Recognition time: Effects of recency, frequency, and the spacing of repetitions. *Journal of Experimental Psychology, 79*, 192–194.

Hintzman, D. L. (1974). Theoretical implications of the spacing effect. In R. L. Solso (Ed.), *Theories in cognitive psychology: The Loyola symposium* (pp. 77–97). Potomac: Erlbaum.

Horowitz, H. M. (1988). Student response systems. In *Proceedings of the 6th Annual Conference on Interactive Instruction Delivery, Society for Applied Learning Technology.* Warrenton, VA.

Jonassen, D. H., & Grabowski, B. L. (1993). *Handbook of individual differences, learning, and instruction.* Hillsdale, NJ: Erlbaum.

Kahana, M. J., & Howard, M. W. (2005). Spacing and lag effects in free recall of pure lists. *Psychonomic Bulletin & Review, 12*, 159–164.

Kang, S. H. K. (2016). Spaced repetition promotes efficient and effective learning: Policy implications for instruction. *Policy Insights from the Behavioral and Brain Sciences, 3*(1), 12–19.

Knight, J. K., & Wood, W. B. (2005). Teaching more by lecturing less. *CBE Life Science Education, 4*, 298–310.

Lee, T. D., & Genovese, E. D. (1988). Distribution of practice in motor skill acquisition: Learning and performance effects reconsidered. *Research Quarterly, 59*, 277–287.

Lent, R. C. (2012). *Overcoming textbook fatigue: 21st century tools to revitalize teaching and learning.* Alexandria, VA: Association for Supervision and Curriculum Development.

Logan, J. M., Castel, A. D., Haber, S., & Viehman, E. J. (2012). Metacognition and the spacing effect: The role of repetition, feedback, and instruction on judgements of learning for massed spaced rehearsal. *Metacognition Learning, 7*, 175–195.

Macnamara, B. N., Hambrick, D. Z., & Oswald, F. L. (2014). Deliberate practice and performance in music, games, sports, education, and professions: A meta-analysis. *Psychological Science, 25*(8), 1608–1618.

Marzano, R. J. (2004). *Building background knowledge for academic achievement: Research on what works in schools.* Alexandria, VA: Association for Supervision and Curriculum Development.

Mazur, E. (1997). *Peer instruction: A user's manual.* Upper Saddle River, NJ: Prentice Hall.

McClanahan, E. B., & McClanahan, L. L. (2002). Active learning in a non-majors biology class: lessons learned. *College Teaching, 50*, 92–96.

McLeish, J. (1968). *The lecture method* (Vol. 1). Cambridge: Cambridge Institute of Education.

Melton, A. W. (1970). The situation with respect to the spacing of repetitions and memory. *Journal of Verbal Learning & Verbal Behavior, 9*, 596–606.

Pasley, J. D., Weiss, I. R., Shimkus, S. P., & Smith, P. S. (2004). Looking inside the classroom: Science teaching in the United States. *Science Educator, 13*, 1–12.

Powell, K. (2003). Spare me the lecture. *Nature, 425*, 234–236.

Pressley, M., Wood, E., Woloshyn, V. E., & Martin, V. (1992). Encouraging mindful use of prior knowledge: Attempting to construct explanatory answers facilitates learning. *Educational Psychologist, 27*(1), 91–109.

Rowe, D.W., & Rayford, L. (1987). Activating background knowledge in reading comprehension assessment. *Reading Research Quarterly, 22*(2), 160–176.

Ruch, T. C. (1928). Factors influencing the relative economy of massed and distributed practice in learning. *Psychological Review, 35*, 19–45.

Son, L. K., & Simon, D. A. (2012). Distributed learning: Data, metacognition, and educational implications. *Educational Psychology Review, 24*, 379–399.

Spires, H. A., & Donley, J. (1998). Prior knowledge activation: Inducing engagement with informational texts. *Journal of Educational Psychology, 90*(2), 249–260.

Stevens, K. C. (1980). The effect of background knowledge on the reading comprehension of ninth graders. *Journal of Reading Behavior, 12*(2), 151–154.

Strangman, N., Hall, T., & Meyer, A. (2004). *Background knowledge instruction and the implications for UDL implementation.* Wakefield, MA: National Center on Accessing the General Curriculum.

Stuart, J., & Rutherford, R. J. (1978). Medical student concentration during lectures. *The Lancet, 2*, 514–516.

Toto, J., & Booth, K. (2008). Effects and implications of mini-lectures on learning in first-semester general chemistry. *Chemistry Education Research and Practice, 9*, 259–266.

Verkoeijen, P. P. J. L., Rikers, R. M. J. P., & Özsoy, B. (2008). Distributed rereading can hurt the spacing effect in text memory. *Applied Cognitive Psychology, 22*, 685–695.

Wahlheim, C. N., Maddox, G. B., & Jacoby, L. L. (2014). The role of reminding in the effects of spaced repetitions on cued recall: Sufficient but not necessary. *Journal of Experimental Psychology: Learning, Memory, and Cognition, 40*, 94–105.

Walker, J. D., Cotner, S. H., Baepler, P. M., & Decker, M. D. (2008). A delicate balance: Integrating active learning into a large lecture course. *CBE Life Sciences Education, 7*, 361–367.

Wankat, P. (2002). *The effective efficient professor: Teaching, scholarship and service.* Boston, MA: Allyn and Bacon.

Young, J. R. (2008). Short and sweet: Technology shrinks the lecture. *The Chronicle of Higher Education: Information Technology, 54*(41), A9.

Credits

CHAPTER 4

Engaging Students Through Independent and Small Group Work

KEY CONCEPTS IN THE CHAPTER:

- Different teaching styles in research methods
- Independent work strategies
- Group work strategies
- Examples and tips

As instructors, most of us have probably asked students to introduce themselves the first day of class and to state why they chose to enroll in the course. Most of us, however, probably do not use this exercise in our research methods courses because we know most (possibly even all) of the students' responses will be "because it is required." This response is probably more common in research methods than any other course students take as part of their social science major requirements.

Most students are just not excited about research methods; they view it as an obstacle they must endure in order to receive their degrees.

The additional challenges faced by research methods instructors is termed by Briggs, Brown, Gardner, and Davidson (2009) as D.RA.MA, referring to student disinterest (D), students' view that research methods is not relevant to them and their career goals (RA), and math anxiety (MA). They argue that students find the subject matter to be dull and uninteresting. Students also do not believe the knowledge they derive from research methods will be useful to them in their professional careers after college. These issues are confounded with students' concerns that the course is difficult. Given these challenges facing research methods instructors, it is important to move beyond traditional teaching strategies and incorporate several varied techniques to make research methods more enjoyable to students, and to you as the instructor. This chapter discusses several independent and group active learning techniques that instructors can utilize, as well as specific examples of these techniques and helpful tips.

Types of Active Learning

The past couple of decades have seen a surge of interest in various teaching methods among college faculty to better engage students, outside of the traditional lecture mode. Briefly introduced in Chapter 3, active learning is a general instructional method that engages students in the learning process and makes them more aware of how knowledge is constructed (Bonwell & Eison, 1991; Eison, 2010; Faust & Paulson, 1998; Meyers & Jones, 1993; Silberman, 1996; Van Hout-Wolters, Simons, & Volet, 2000). Instead of the instructor lecturing throughout the entire class period, students are encouraged to weigh in and have conversations about the material through various activities such as comparing notes during class, short writing exercises, small group work, listening practices, etc. (Faust & Paulson, 1998; McKeachie, 2002; Prince, 2004). It can involve students working independently on tasks related to course content or with others (e.g., peer-to-peer or small group work) on collaborative activities that reflect different peer perspectives (Eyt-Dessus, 2017). It can also involve both formal and informal strategies, depending on the class dynamics, the content being learned, and the instructor's preference (Cueso, 1992). Formal group work (e.g., team-based projects) generally incorporates the instructor choosing the makeup of the group, which helps to maximize heterogeneity and diversity of perspectives, as well as enhance group interdependence (Cueso, 1992; Garfield, 1993; Johnson & Johnson, 1999; Johnson, Johnson, & Smith, 1991). Informal strategies (e.g., think-pair-share/write-pair-share) may be easier for instructors to integrate into lecture because it does not require a lot of prior work, exercises usually only take a few minutes, and there is typically no expectation of work to be turned in or graded (Cooper & Robinson, 2000; Garfield, 1993; Johnson et al., 1991).

Proponents of active learning suggest that this type of teaching style helps to break up the monotony of traditional lectures and focus students' attention (Prince, 2004). Wankat (2002) offers several studies that propose that a student's attention span during lectures is approximately 15 minutes. Following that, attention decreases drastically, resulting in a loss in retention of the course material (Bligh, 2000; Burns, 1985; Hartley & Davies, 1978; Stuart & Rutherford, 1978). Active learning allows the possibility to break up the lecture period and keep student's minds active, engaged, and able to retain a larger portion of the material.

We learned in Chapter 3 the advantages of incorporating active learning methods; yet, various forms of this teaching style exist. Instructors can decide which method will be most beneficial to their class. As active learning can incorporate both individual and small group work, collaborative learning provides a teaching method where students work together in small groups (usually of three or more) toward a common goal. There is an emphasis on social interactions rather than solitary activity, creating an exchange of ideas and perspectives that encourages critical thinking, motivation, and retention of information (Gokhale, 1995). Scholars have revealed several benefits of collaborative learning with small group work, such as increased understanding of course material; improved self-esteem and responsibility; the development of higher-level thinking, oral communication, and leadership skills; the promotion of student–faculty interaction; improved feedback; and a better ability to understand different perspectives (Johnson & Johnson, 1986; Johnson, Johnson, & Smith, 1998a, 1998b; Springer, Stanne, & Donovan, 1999). For this type of teaching style to be effective, the instructor must take on the role of a facilitator rather than one who transmits information. It is important to view teaching as a process of development and enhancement of students' abilities to learn through stimulation and interactions (Barr & Tagg, 1995; De Hei, Strijbos, Sjoer, & Admiraal, 2015; Garfield, 1993; Gokhale, 1995). By doing this, collaborative techniques can facilitate active learning and promote retention by increasing contact among diverse groups (Bossert, 1988; Bowman, Frame, & Kennette, 2013; Hennessey, 1999; Kennette & Frank, 2013; Kramarski & Mevarech, 2003; Rajaram & Pereira-Pasarin, 2007; U.S. Department of Education, 1992).

Lastly, cooperative learning is a specific type of collaborative learning where students work together in small groups on a structured activity (Artzt & Newman, 1990; Felder & Brent, 2007; Johnson & Johnson, 1999). Students are held individually accountable for their efforts, while also being assessed as a whole for the work of the group (Johnson et al., 1998). This type of learning stresses cooperative incentives rather than competition between students (Johnson, Johnson, & Stanne, 2000). Groups can either be informal, where students choose the group members, or more formal, where the instructor creates the group makeup (Garfield, 1993). Students then work together to solve a problem, complete a task, or accomplish a common goal (Johnson, Johnson, & Holubec, 1998). By incorporating cooperative learning, students ultimately teach each other concepts and ideas, positive interdependence is promoted, communication is enhanced, students can comprehend there is more than one way to solve a problem, and students have more of an opportunity to ask questions and understand the material better (Felder & Brent, 2007; Johnson & Johnson, 1989, 1999; Johnson et al., 1991; McKeachie, Pintrich, Yi-Guang, & Smith, 1986).

Independent Work

Active learning methods have the ability to integrate both individual tasks and small group work. Independent work allows students to think things through on their own, creating a more comfortable atmosphere to process information. According to Gokhale (1995), collaborative learning through individual tasks is very effective in gaining factual knowledge. Instructors can introduce student activity into traditional lectures fairly easily, and with little preparation using either low-stakes or no-stakes (i.e., not graded) assessments (Faust & Paulson, 1998; Johnston & Cooper, 1997; King,

1993; Meyers & Jones, 1993; Silberman, 1996). This can provide an effective means of communication between the student and the instructor, especially in larger classes where it can be difficult to develop rapport (Faust & Paulson, 1998).

INDEPENDENT WORK FOR LEARNING VARIABLES

Distribute worksheets listing several hypotheses. Provide students time during class to read over the hypotheses and identify the dependent and independent variables for each one. Give them plenty of time to complete it, remembering that some students will work faster than others. Walk around the room and assist students who are struggling. Once the students have completed the worksheet, review the correct answers with the entire class, allowing students to "grade" their own papers. This exercise should not be done as a graded assignment; it should only be used to allow students to assess their own knowledge. After reviewing the answers, encourage students who struggled to seek assistance from you. It is also a good idea to provide additional copies of the worksheet on a course management system so students can use them to assess their own knowledge when preparing for exams or quizzes.

Turning Point/Clickers

The audience response technique using technology is a great way for instructors with a large class size to encourage students to participate actively in the lecture. Students respond to several questions posed during a PowerPoint presentation by pressing a button on their clicker. The correct answer is then revealed, along with a breakdown of student responses (Caldwell, 2007). This allows the instructor to gather feedback instantly on the retention of course material, and to easily gauge group-wide understanding/misunderstanding (Caldwell, 2007; Draper, Cargill, Cutts, 2002; Wood, 2004). Turning points are particularly easy to use because they require minimal preparation for the instructor, and there is no manual grading to be done (Brewer, 2004; Parsons, 2005; Roschelle, Penuel, &

Abrahamson, 2004). Furthermore, it helps to break up the lecture and keep students' attention (Cooper & Robinson, 2000).

TIP: GRADING TURNING POINT RESPONSES IN RESEARCH METHODS

We recommend that instructors use automatic response systems simply as a gauge of students' comprehension. It is important, however, to award points to students' participation in the activity or several students will likely elect not to participate. In order to relieve student anxiety, you want to avoid requiring students to get the answer correct to receive points. Systems can be set up so students receive a point for each click regardless of whether their response is correct or incorrect. This still allows you to determine whether more time needs to be spent on a specific topic while avoiding penalizing students who are still struggling with the material. If graded this way, it also eliminates the need to take attendance in your classes. We further recommend a grading scale based on percentage of clicks. This way when a student forgets his or her clicker it will not affect his or her grade as long as the student does not forget it too often. We provide a sample syllabus summary and grading scale below:

> Participation will be assessed based on your responses to clicker questions during the class period. Regardless of whether your response is correct or incorrect you will be given credit for each time you participate. Grading will be determined by your percentage of participation. Clicker points cannot be made-up. If you miss class or forget your clicker, you will not get points that day.
>
> 100–80% = 30 points
> 79–70% = 25 points
> 69–60% = 20 points
> 59–50% = 15 points
> 49–40% = 10 points
> 39–30% = 5 points
> Less than 30% = 0 points

Clarification Pause

Clarification pauses are a very simple way to encourage active listening, and to increase the students' attention span throughout the lecture. Rowe (1980) illustrated this in suggesting that pausing in between lectures every 13 to 28 minutes will significantly increase student attention and learning. Clarification pauses help students to review their notes, reflect on them, and discuss concepts with the class (Bachhel & Thaman, 2014). Throughout the lecture, the instructor stops talking after introducing an important concept to let the material sink in. After waiting a short period for students to reflect, the instructor asks if anyone has any questions or needs anything to be clarified further (Faust & Paulson, 1998). This process also helps to avoid the common problem throughout traditional lectures of information "going in one ear and out the other" (Johnson et al., 1991).

CLARIFICATION PAUSE COUPLED WITH EXAMPLES IN RESEARCH METHODS

After a clarification pause, review some examples that allow students to apply the knowledge they just learned during the lecture before proceeding to a new topic. For example, after reviewing units of analysis, present students with a simple hypothesis. Consider the following examples:

> Communities with higher rates of unemployment have higher rates of crime than communities with lower rates of unemployment.
>
> Juveniles who live in high-crime areas are more likely to be stopped by the police than juveniles who live in low-crime areas.
>
> Offenders with addiction issues who attend drug treatment court have lower recidivism rates than offenders with addiction issues who receive jail time.

After giving students a few seconds to read the hypothesis, ask them to identify the unit of analysis. Do this for a few different hypotheses with various units of analysis.

Muddiest/Clearest Point

The muddiest/clearest point process requires instructors to have students spend the last several minutes of class responding to the questions: "What concept did you find the most challenging in today's class?" and "What concept do you feel you have a clear understanding of from today's class?" (Angelo & Cross, 1993; Faust & Paulson, 1998). The instructor then collects the responses and reviews them before the next class period. This is beneficial because it can help the instructor determine gaps in student retention, and then set aside time for the next class period to review material that was not understood clearly (Angelo & Cross, 1993). It also aids the students because it allows them to recognize where they are struggling with the course material. They can then direct their learning efforts to that specific misunderstanding, and better engage in deeper learning (Yasuhara, 2015).

MUDDIEST/CLEAREST POINT FOR CONCEPTUALIZATION AND OPERATIONAL DEFINITIONS

The muddiest/clearest point strategy can be used at the conclusion of every class. In research methods, you might find it is especially useful when teaching about the process to measure concepts. Students typically struggle with developing conceptualizations and operational definitions that can be used to develop a technique to measure concepts. A quick assessment is helpful before moving on to new material.

Minute Paper

Similar to the muddiest/clearest point strategy, the minute paper is a very common assessment technique used by many disciplines to motivate students to reflect on the material learned throughout a given lecture period (Angelo & Cross, 1993). It also provides a source of faculty-student communication, which can be difficult to achieve with larger classes. Students spend the last several minutes of class (or can pause at some point during the lecture) answering a question that has been posed by the instructor related to the material presented in lecture. This can be anything from "What was the main point presented in today's class?" to "What concept did you find the most difficult to understand from the material today?" (Faust & Paulson, 1998; Wilson, 1986). It is also possible to spend the first several minutes of the class answering a question related to homework assignments (Cooper & Robinson, 2000). In this sense, the minute paper can act as a form of in-class quizzing, which will further be explained during Chapter 7. These responses give immediate feedback to the instructor on student retention and gaps within the learning process. Furthermore, students can either submit their responses with their names on them (if used in the form of a quiz) or anonymously. Anonymous responses can permit students to feel more comfortable voicing a concern with the material; however, it can also allow the possibility for students to feel they do not have to put as much thought into their response (Faust & Paulson, 1998; Harwood, 1996). It is important for instructors to gauge their class and determine the best course of action.

A MINUTE PAPER IN RESEARCH METHODS ETHICS

After completing a lecture on ethnical concerns in research methods and the safeguards researchers should put in place to protect their subjects, show the documentary *Quiet Rage: The Stanford Prison Experiment*, which explains Phillip Zimbardo's controversial study on inmate and guard behavior. Allow students to take notes on the ethical violations they observe during the documentary. After the documentary, ask them to reflect on what the researcher should have done to protect his subjects from these ethical violations. After students have written down their thoughts, ask them to share their thoughts with the class. You can also require the students to hand in the assignment for credit. This assignment will allow you to gauge students' understanding of ethical issues and safeguards by requiring them to apply these concepts to a real-life research example.

Small Group Work

Engaging students through active learning can be a great way to enhance a traditional lecture and promote deep learning. While the use of individual tasks to accomplish this can be quick and easy, utilizing small group work throughout the semester can contribute even more to the learning process. Evidence presented by Johnson and Johnson (1986) suggests that small group work can promote higher levels of retention for longer periods of time than individual work alone. Other scholars have found similar results as well, demonstrating that students who participate in collaborative group learning perform significantly better on critical-thinking tests, problem-solving strategies, and overall academic achievement (Bruner, 1985; Freeman et al., 2014; Gokhale, 1995; Norman & Schmidt, 2000; Vygotsky, 1978). Furthermore, the use of small group allows for group diversity with regards to both knowledge and experience, which can contribute significantly to the learning process (Gokhale, 1995). Students can not only hear different perspectives related to a specific topic, but they can share their own opinion on the matter as well. This helps improve listening and communication skills, positive interdependence, exposure to/understanding new perspectives, the development of higher-level thinking, and an increase in retention (Garfield, 1993).

GROUP WORK EXERCISE: CONCEPTUALIZATIONS, OPERATIONAL DEFINITIONS, AND MEASUREMENTS

Break students into small groups of three to four students. Provide them with the following hypothesis: Communities with high poverty rates experience higher rates of serious crime. Direct them to (1) identify the concepts in the hypothesis (communities, high poverty rates, and serious crime), (2) develop conceptualizations for each concept, (3) develop operational definitions for each concept, and (4) develop measurements for the independent and dependent variable concepts. Give the students 25 to 30 minutes to complete the exercise. When the groups are finished, ask them to share their work with the whole class. During the class discussion ask the other students to discuss the strengths and weaknesses of the other groups' work to encourage critical thinking and to illustrate how difficult it is to create the "perfect" measure of a concept.

Think-Pair-Share/Write-Pair-Share

Think-pair-share/write-pair-share is an informal activity that often begins with information that has already been provided to the students through a short lecture, reading assignment, or visual presentation (Eison, 2010). The instructor then poses a question or problem to the class, and students take a few minutes to either think about or write down an answer individually. Afterwards, students can either turn to a partner or form small groups and discuss their answers (Cooper & Robinson, 2000; Kaddoura, 2013). By doing so, students have the opportunity to share their views on a topic, hear perspectives from others, engage in higher-level thinking, understand why they answered the question either correctly or incorrectly, and have the ability to teach other students about a concept of which they may have a better understanding (Cooper & Robinson, 2000; Shakarian, 1995). As a conclusion to this activity, it is often beneficial to have the group then respond to the entire class. This provides a meaningful discussion amongst all students, and it allows both the instructor and the students to receive immediate feedback on the retention of the material (Cooper & Robinson, 2000). The instructor can subsequently either move on to the next part of the lecture or spend more time on the material that students found the most challenging.

LEARNING RESEARCH DESIGNS

Create four different scenarios depicting a research problem. One example could be:

> County X has decided to implement a new drunk driving initiative in an effort to reduce recidivism rates of individuals convicted of drunk driving. The program provides treatment and education to those receiving their first drunk driving offense. The county has been facilitating the program for 1 year. They have asked you, as a researcher, to conduct research to determine whether their program is effective. Identify the strongest research design possible to determine whether their program is effective in reducing recidivism for first-time drunk driving offenders.

Distribute one problem to each student (multiple students will have the same problem). Ask each student to read the problem and decide which research design would be the strongest design to answer the research questions. For this portion, each student should work individually. Once students have thought through the problem and identified the best design on their own, ask students to find the other members in the class who have the same design and get into a group with those students. In those small groups, each student should share the design they picked and explain why they determined that to be the strongest design. The group should next decide which one design, from the different designs each individual student picked, is the best one. The group will then be directed to share their research question, design, and reasons for picking that design with the whole class.

Study Groups

Study group work generally occurs outside of class, and can be a beneficial way for instructors to incorporate small group work into their teaching style, yet still allow for enough time in lecture to cover the material. Scholars have proposed that study groups have the ability to increase academic achievement, improve confidence in course material, enhance communication skills, and increase understanding of new perspectives (Petress, 2004).

Study groups can be used throughout the semester for students to prepare for exams or quizzes or simply to review concepts presented throughout lecture. Generally, study groups should contain between three to six individuals so that organization can remain manageable and it can be assured that enough material will be covered (Barkley, Cross, & Major, 2005). Study groups are generally self-formed, and the time, location, and duration of the group is up to the members involved to decide (Rybczynski & Schussler, 2011). These meetings can then be used for sharing lecture notes, reviewing course content, and discussing any gaps in understanding. It may be helpful for the instructor to periodically check in with each study group to see if any material needs to be reviewed that remains confusing to any group members.

STUDY GROUPS

It can be difficult to encourage students to get together outside of class to study. With different work, home, and school schedules, students are not always available to study at the same time. Encouraging many sessions on different days and times can help. Do not restrict students to one group. Instead allow them to attend any session for which they are available. Extra credit points can also be used to encourage participation. A good strategy is to base points on percentage of sessions attended. For example, students who attend 85% or more sessions get 5 extra credit points on the exam, those who attend 70% to 84% receive 3 extra credit points on the exam, and so on. The number of extra credit points will vary by the point breakdown and difficulty of your class. However, the points should be assigned to an upcoming assignment or exam and not accumulative over the course of the semester. This will improve retention by allowing students who did not take advantage of the sessions early in the semester to do so later in the semester. These shorter-term rewards will also help keep students motivated to continue attending the sessions. It is also a good idea to check with your university or department to see if funds are available to hire an upper-level or graduate student to facilitate these study sessions.

Team-Based Projects

Team-based projects are often more formal and structured, where students work toward accomplishing a more comprehensive array of course material (Faust & Paulson, 1998; Sharan & Sharan, 1994). Instructors generally determine the size and composition of the group, where it is beneficial to form heterogeneous groups (i.e., varying learning styles, GPAs, majors, personalities, ages, gender, ethnic backgrounds, class standing, etc.) (Cooper et al., 1990; Cueso, 1992; Faust & Paulson, 1998; Smith, 1996). This can have both positive and negative consequences. By forming groups of such diversity, there is a likelihood that some group members may not get along or feel comfortable, which can hinder group performance and success. On the other hand, heterogeneity and diversity of perspectives can enhance group performance and supportive relationships because students are able to form bonds throughout the duration of the project, hear different interpretations of a problem, and ultimately improve their problem-solving strategies by working through different perspectives to accomplish a common goal (Bruner, 1985; Slavin, 1994).

Team-based projects generally include a single group grade that is assigned to all members of the group at the completion of the assignment. A common issue that arises with this method is that one or two students end up doing all of the work, with other members putting forth little effort (yet still receiving the same grade) (Cueso, 1992). This finding has been supported by other scholars who contend that efforts produced by students will decrease when they are placed in a group, unless the output of each student is uniquely identifiable (Williams, Harkins, & Latane, 1981). Therefore, individual accountability needs to be integrated into the final project grade in order to best achieve deeper learning. For example, projects can be broken down into smaller assignments that are set at multiple deadlines, and both individual and group grades can be assigned to each segment (Cueso, 1992; Felder & Brent, 2007). Both assessment scores (individual and final group) are then used to determine the student's course grade (Michaelsen, Knight, & Fink, 2004). This method allows for individual incentives and grades that also motivate the overall well-being of the final group product. Additionally, multiple deadlines ensures that students are reaching milestones throughout the process, rather than pulling a product together at the last minute (Cueso, 1992).

TEAM-BASED PROJECT FOR DEVELOPING A TESTABLE RESEARCH QUESTION

Early in the semester, ask students to complete a short questionnaire indicating which area of the criminal justice system they are most interested in. Review the results of the questionnaire and place students with similar interest into small groups. You can also do the opposite and group students together with different interests; however, given the difficulty and purpose of this assignment, we recommended placing students with similar interest together. Direct students to identify a current issue in their area of interest. After the group members have decided on a current issue, direct each group member to find a peer-reviewed article on the topic and write a summary of the article. For this portion of the assignment, students must work independently. Each student should then share his or her findings with the group and submit the summary and article to be graded. Each student will receive an individual grade for his or her review. After all the group members have shared their reviews, the groups will work together to develop their own research questions based on the literature they reviewed. One set of research questions will be submitted for the group, so the group members must work together to develop the questions based on the knowledge each member brings from the individual article summaries.

Summary

Because of the special challenges with student interests and anxieties that teaching research methods presents, it is important that instructors move beyond the traditional lecture format. Students learn research methods best when they apply it to examples, have time to think through the concepts, and assist each other. The techniques presented in this chapter incorporate all of these things and will make the class more interesting for students. From our experiences, however, we find that the positives greatly outweigh the negatives. Although you might have a student or two who feels that using class time for independent work and group activities is a waste of time, the majority of the students will learn more, earn better scores in the class, and will enjoy class time more because these techniques are incorporated. For the student who wishes not to participate in nongraded activities, we have found it best not to force him or her but simply ask the student to sit quietly and not disturb other students. (From 10 years of teaching this course, the few students who have decided to take that option have changed their minds after receiving their first exam scores.)

Additional pitfalls arise with graded group work. Issues surrounding fair division of work, different levels of motivation, conflicting schedules, personality differences, varying work ethic, and different standards of quality coursework all complicate group assignments. Many instructors require students to work through these issues with the justification that students will have to work with others in their professional careers. Other strategies are also possible. One is to require some individual effort and work to be part of the group assignment (see our example in the team-based project section). For these parts of the projects, students' grades are independent. It is also a good idea to require groups to document each member's individual contribution. This can even be taken a step further, where part of each person's grade is based on the other group members' assessment of their contribution. Even with these strategies, instructors have to be prepared to deal with group conflicts and disagreements when students must complete work for a grade. The best way to avoid them is to reserve group work for assignments that are not graded. When avoided, however, students lose the opportunity to learn from managing these conflicts, a task they will inevitably have to do during their professional careers.

References

Angelo, T. A., & Cross, K. P. (1993). *Classroom assessment techniques* (2nd ed.). San Francisco, CA: Jossey-Bass.

Artzt, A., & Newman, C. (1990). *How to use cooperative learning in the mathematics class.* Reston, VA: National Council of Teachers of Mathematics.

Bachhel, R., & Thaman, R.G. (2014). Effective use of pause procedure to enhance student engagement and learning. *Journal of Clinical & Diagnostic Research, 8*(8), XM01-XM03.

Barkley, E. F., Cross, K. P., & Major, C. H. (2005). *Collaborative learning techniques: A handbook for college faculty.* San Francisco, CA: Jossey-Bass.

Barr, R. B., & Tagg, J. (1995). From teaching to learning—A new paradigm for undergraduate education. *Change: The Magazine of Higher Learning, 27*(6), 13–25.

Bligh, D. A. (2000). *What's the use of lectures?* San Francisco, CA: Jossey-Bass.

Bonwell, C. C., & Eison, J. A. (1991). *Active learning: Creating excitement in the classroom* (ASHE-ERIC Higher Education Report No. 1). Washington, DC: Association for the Study of Higher Education.

Bossert, S. T. (1988). Cooperative activities in the classroom. *Review of Research in Education, 15,* 225–250.

Bowman, M., Frame, D. L., & Kennette, L. N. (2013). Enhancing teaching and learning: How cognitive research can help. *Journal on Excellence in College Teaching: Brain-Based Learning* (Special Issue), *24*(3), 7–28.

Brewer, C. (2004). Near real-time assessment of student learning and understanding in biology courses. *BioScience, 54*(11), 1034–1039.

Briggs, L. S., Brown, S. E., Gardner, R. B., & Davidson, R. L. (2009). D.RA.MA: An extended conceptualization of student anxiety in criminal justice research methods courses. *Journal of Criminal Justice Education, 20*(3), 217–226.

Bruner, J. (1985). Vygotsky: An historical and conceptual perspective. In J. W. Wertsch (Ed.), *Culture, communication, and cognition: Vygotskian perspectives* (pp. 21–34). London: Cambridge University Press.

Burns, R. A. (1985). *Information impact and factors affecting recall.* Presented at Annual National Conference on Teaching Excellence and Conference of Administrators, Austin, TX.

Caldwell, J. E. (2007). Clickers in the large classroom: Current research and best-practice tips. *CBE Life Sciences Education, 6*, 9–20.

Cooper, J., Prescott, J. S., Cook, L., Smith, L., Mueck, R., & Cuseo, J. (1990). *Cooperative learning and college instruction: Effective use of student learning teams.* Long Beach: California State University Foundation.

Cooper, J. L., & Robinson, P. (2000). Getting started: Informal small-group strategies in large classes. *New Directions for Teaching and Learning, 81*, 17–24.

Cueso, J. (1992). Cooperative learning vs. small-group discussions and group projects: The critical differences. *Cooperative Learning and College Teaching, 2*(3), 5–10.

De Hei, M. S. A., Strijbos, J. W., Sjoer, E., & Admiraal, W. (2015). Collaborative learning in higher education: Lecturers' practices and beliefs. *Research Papers in Education, 30*(2), 232–247.

Draper, S., Cargill, J., & Cutts, Q. (2002). Electronically enhanced classroom interaction. *Australasian Journal of Educational Technology, 18*(1), 13–23.

Eison, J. (2010). Using active learning instructional strategies to create excitement and enhance learning. University of South Florida, Department of Adult, Career, & Higher Education. Retrieved from *file:///F:/Book%20Proposal/Articles/Eison_Active%20Learning.pdf*

Eyt-Dessus, A. (2017, April 24). Active and collaborative learning. Retrieved July 26, 2017, from https://sleguidance.atlassian.net/wiki/display/CL/Active+and+Collaborative+Learning

Faust, J. L., & Paulson, D. R. (1998). Active learning in the college classroom. *Journal on Excellence in College Teaching, 9*(2), 3–24.

Felder, R. M., & Brent, R. (2007). Cooperative learning. In P. A. Mabrouk (Ed.), *Active learning: Models from the analytical sciences* (pp. 34–53). Washington, DC: American Chemical Society.

Freeman, S., Eddy, S. L., McDonough, M., Smith, M. K., Okoroafor, N., Jordt, H., & Wenderoth, M. P. (2014). Active learning increases student performance in science, engineering, and mathematics. *Proceedings of the National Academy of Sciences, USA, 111*(23), 8410–8415.

Garfield, J. (1993). Teaching statistics using small-group cooperative learning. *Journal of Statistics Education, 1*(1).

Gokhale, A. A. (1995). Collaborative learning enhances critical thinking. *Journal of Technology Education, 7*(1).

Hartley, J., & Davies, I. (1978). Note-taking: A critical review. *Programmed Learning and Educational Technology, 15*(3), 207–224.

Harwood, W. S. (1996). The one-minute paper: A communication tool for large lecture classes. *Journal of Chemical Education, 73*, 229–230.

Hennessey, M. G. (1999). Probing the dimensions of metacognition: Implications for conceptual change teaching-learning. Paper presented at the annual meeting of the National Association for Research in Science Teaching, Boston, MA. Retrieved from http://eric.ed.gov/PDFS/ED446921.pdf

Johnson, D. W., & Johnson, R. (1989). *Cooperation and competition: Theory and research.* Edina, MN: Interaction Book.

Johnson, D. W., & Johnson, R.T. (1999). Making cooperative learning work. *Theory into Practice, 38*(2), 67–73.

Johnson, D. W., Johnson, R., & Holubec, E. (1998). *Cooperation in the classroom* (7th ed.). Edina, MN: Interaction Book.

Johnson, D. W., Johnson, R. T., & Smith, K. (1991). *Cooperative learning: Increasing college faculty instructional productivity* (ASHE-ERIC Higher Education Report No. 4). Washington, DC: Association for the Study of Higher Education.

Johnson, D., Johnson, R., & Smith, K. (1998a). *Active learning: Cooperation in the college classroom* (2nd ed.). Edina, MN: Interaction Book.

Johnson, D., Johnson, R., & Smith, K. (1998b). Cooperative learning returns to college: What evidence is there that it works? *Change: The Magazine of Higher Learning, 30*(4), 26–35.

Johnson, D. W., Johnson, R. T., & Stanne, M. E. (2000). Cooperative learning methods: A meta-analysis. University of Minnesota, MN, Cooperative Learning Center. Retrieved from http://www.cooperation.org/pages/cl-methods.html

Johnson, R. T., & Johnson, D. W. (1986). Action research: Cooperative learning in the science classroom. *Science and Children, 24*, 31–32.

Johnston, S., & Cooper, J. (1997). Quick thinks: Active-learning tasks in lecture classes and televised instruction. *Cooperative Learning and College Teaching, 8*(1), 3–5.

Kaddoura, M. (2013). Think pair share: A teaching learning strategy to enhance students' critical thinking. *Educational Research Quarterly, 36*(4), 3–24.

Kennette, L. N., & Frank, N. M. (2013). The value of peer-review opportunities for students in writing-intensive classes. *Psychology Teaching Review, 19*(2), 106–111.

King, A. (1993). From sage on the stage to guide on the side. *College Teaching, 41*(1), 30–35.

Kramarski, B., & Mevarech, Z. R. (2003). Enhancing mathematical reasoning in the classroom: The effects of cooperative learning and metacognitive training. *American Educational Research Journal, 40*(1), 281–310.

McKeachie, W. J. (2002). *Teaching tips: Strategies, research, and theory for college and university teachers* (11th ed.). Boston, MA: Houghton Mifflin.

McKeachie, W., Pintrich, P., Yi-Guang, L., & Smith, D. (1986). *Teaching and learning in the college classroom: A review of the research literature.* Ann Arbor: Regents of the University of Michigan.

Meyers, C., & Jones, T. (1993). *Promoting active learning: Strategies for the college classroom.* San Francisco, CA: Jossey-Bass.

Michaelsen, L. K., Knight, A. B. & Fink, L. D. (2004). *Team-based learning: A transformative use of small groups in college teaching.* Sterling, VA: Stylus.

Norman, G., & Schmidt, H. (2000). Effectiveness of problem-based learning curricula: Theory, practice and paper darts. *Medical Education, 34,* 721–728.

Parsons, C. V. (2005). Decision making in the process of differentiation. *Learning and Leading with Technology, 33*(1), 8–10.

Petress, K. C. (2004). The benefits of group study. *Education, 124,* 587–589.

Prince, M. (2004). Does active learning work? A review of the research. *Journal of Engineering Education, 93*(3), 223–231.

Rajaram, S., & Pereira-Pasarin, L. P. (2007). Collaboration can improve individual recognition memory: Evidence from immediate and delayed tests. *Psychonomic Bulletin & Review, 14*(1), 95–100.

Roschelle, J., Penuel, W. R., & Abrahamson, L. (2004). Classroom response and communication systems: Research review and theory. Presented at the Annual Meeting of the American Educational Research Association, San Diego, CA.

Rowe, M. (1980). Pausing principles and their effects on reasoning in science. In F. Brawer (Ed.), *Teaching the sciences: New directions for community colleges (pp. 27–34).* San Francisco, CA: Jossey-Bass.

Rybczynski, S. M., & Schussler, E. E. (2011). Student use of out-of-class study groups in an introductory undergraduate biology course. *CBE Life Science Education, 10*(1), 74–82.

Shakarian, D. C. (1995). Beyond lecture: Active-learning strategies that work. *The Journal of Physical Education, Recreation and Dance, 66,* 21–24.

Sharan, Y., & Sharan, S. (1994). Group investigation in the cooperative classroom. In S. Sharan (Ed.), *Handbook of cooperative learning methods* (pp. 97–114). Westport, CT: Greenwood.

Silberman, M. (1996). *Active learning: 101 strategies to teach any subject.* Boston, MA: Allyn and Bacon.

Slavin, R. W. (1994). Student teams-achievement divisions. In S. Sharan (Ed.), *Handbook of cooperative learning methods* (pp. 3–19). Westport, CT: Greenwood.

Smith, K. A. (1996). Cooperative learning: Making "groupwork" work. In T. E. Sutherland & C. C. Bonwell (Eds.), *Using active learning in college classes: A range of options for faculty* (pp. 71–82). New Directions for Teaching and Learning, No. 67. San Francisco, CA: Jossey-Bass.

Springer, L., Stanne, M., & Donovan, S. (1999). Effects of small-group learning on undergraduates in science, mathematics, and engineering and technology: A meta-analysis. *Review of Educational Research, 69*(1), 21–52.

Stuart, J., & Rutherford, R. J. (1978). Medical student concentration during lectures. *The Lancet, 2,* 514–516.

U.S. Department of Education. (1992). Cooperative learning. Office of Research. Retrieved from http://www.ed.gov/pubs/OR/ConsumerGuides/cooplear.html

Van Hout-Wolters, B., Simons, R. J., & Volet, S. (2000). Active learning: Self-directed learning and independent work. In P. R. J. Simons, J. L. van der Linden, & T. Duffy (Eds.), *New learning* (pp. 21–37). Dordrecht: Kluwer.

Vygotsky, L. (1978). *Mind in society: The development of higher psychological processes.* Cambridge, MA: Harvard University Press.

Wankat, P. (2002). *The effective efficient professor: Teaching, scholarship and service.* Boston, MA: Allyn and Bacon.

Williams, K., Harkins, S. G., & Latane, B. (1981). Identifiability as a deterrent to social loafing: Two cheering experiments. *Journal of Personality and Social Psychology, 40*(2), 303–311.

Wilson, R. C. (1986). Improving faculty teaching: Effective use of student evaluations and consultants. *Journal of Higher Education, 57*(2), 192–211.

Wood, W. B. (2004). Clickers: A teaching gimmick that works. *Developmental Cell, 7*(6), 796–798.

Yasuhara, K. (2015, February 2). Muddiest point: Reflecting back to move forward. Retrieved July 26, 2017, from http://www.washington.edu/teaching/2015/02/02/reflecting/

CHAPTER 5

Incorporating Peer-Reviewed Studies into the Class

KEY CONCEPTS IN THE CHAPTER:

- Picking appropriate peer-reviewed studies
- Techniques to help students read and understand scholarly articles
- Assessing students' understanding of the material

Courses in research methods utilize terminology, ideas, and methods that are generally not taught in other criminal justice courses. As such, these courses tend to expose students to scholarly literature and require them to utilize peer-reviewed articles as part of course learning, exercises, and assignments. However, there are many challenges that are presented to students when working with this type of material. Not only do students have difficulties locating and recognizing appropriate peer-reviewed journal articles, but they also have issues reading and understanding the material (Muench, 2000). This is not surprising considering peer-reviewed journal articles are written for experts and incorporate terminology, ideas, methods, and analyses that most college students have not encountered prior to enrolling in the course. When students have difficulties reading these articles, they will likely have problems using the material to develop critiques and complete assignments (MacMillan & MacKenzie, 2012). We often find that students will either choose content from the abstracts or tables or will give their personal opinion on the matter rather than constructing an academic argument (Emmons, Martin, Botts, & Amundson, 2010; Gillen, 2006). It is imperative then that instructors for research methods courses guide students to develop the necessary skills for finding, navigating, and understanding scholarly literature. Peer-reviewed journal articles are powerful tools for stimulating active learning, promoting scientific thinking, and building the capacity to analyze and make credible arguments (Ackerman & Arbour, 2016; Gillen, 2006).

Picking Appropriate Peer-Reviewed Studies

With the advance of technology over the past several decades, a vast amount of information can be found on the Internet. Students and instructors can find both popular and scholarly literature for use on course content and assignments. As such, it is important for students to be able to recognize the differences between the different types of information. An emphasis in research methods courses should be placed on using scholarly journal articles due to their rigorous peer-review process. However, students often have difficulties in properly identifying these sources. Rachal Daigle, and Rachal (2007) found that around 49% of students have difficulty finding the information that is required of them for assignments and papers, as well as distinguishing between scholarly and popular literature. Considering that research methods courses rely on a great deal of information from scholarly sources, there is a need for instructors to take extra steps in building students' capacity to locate and recognize peer-reviewed journal articles.

While it is important for students to be able to find appropriate scholarly articles on their own, it may be good practice to begin by having the instructor select peer-reviewed articles for students to read and utilize for course learning, exercises, and assignments (Rachal et al., 2007). This will help students see what a peer-reviewed journal article may look like once it is time for them to locate one on their own. It is important that instructors select journal articles that are consistent with the goals of the content being taught, as students should be provided with a rationale for how the article and the course content are connected (Biggs, 1999; Finlay & Faulkner, 2010). For instance, if students are learning content related to different sampling techniques, instructors may wish to have students read an article that demonstrates a particular technique taught in class. "A Snowball's Chance in Hell: Doing Fieldwork with Active Residential Burglars" by Wright, Decker, Redfern, and Smith (1992) offers an engaging study that uses snowball sampling to conduct research on active offenders. This article not only draws students in with its' interesting topic, but it guides students through the process and challenges of conducting snowball sampling in real-life settings. Another example related to the course topic of field research may be Homel, Tomsen, and Thommeny's (1992) article, "Public Drinking and Violence: Not Just an Alcohol Problem," where the authors examined the relationship between environmental aspects of public drinking and the occurrence of violence. Through this article, students are taught another method of sampling, as well as additional content related to field research (e.g., conducting and recording observations, roles of the researcher, advantages and challenges of field research, etc.). It is important for instructors to choose scholarly articles that will prompt students' interest and connect with content that is learned in class.

Once the instructor has preselected articles for class discussion, it is a good idea to have students understand how to select their own appropriate peer-reviewed journal articles. Being able to locate journal articles on their own will help students understand how to decipher different types of literature and identify credible sources. Considering the amount of information that is available online today, it is important for instructors to provide guidance and insight in finding and recognizing peer-reviewed journal articles (Fujimoto, Hagel, Turner, Kattiyapornpong, & Zutshi, 2011). This can be done in several ways, including instructions given directly from the instructor or scheduling an informational session through the university's library. If instructors cannot fit this into their course schedule, another option may be to assign students to listen to a podcast or video outside of class that will walk them through the process of finding and recognizing scholarly journal articles (Cowie, 2012a, 2012b). With this option, instructors should pair the video with an exercise or assignment that will allow them to know whether students were able to comprehend and apply the information correctly.

Regardless of the instructional method used, students should be guided through different types of literature, as well as where to find that literature. Instructors should teach students the difference between popular versus scholarly literature, as well as between original research and reviews of literature (American Psychological Association, n.d.; Cowie, 2012a). Moreover, students should be taught how to recognize whether a given piece of information is a "peer-reviewed journal article." Often, students will utilize newspaper or magazine articles for class papers and assignments because they are readily available and easy to read. However, this type of literature is written by reporters who may or may not be experts in the field (Library Guides, n.d.). Students also may easily find and use journal articles that are written by academics and professionals but are not "peer reviewed." While this type of information is more credible than some newspaper and magazine articles, these articles have not been peer reviewed, and may still present inaccurate or extreme ideas (Library Guides, n.d.). Instead, students should utilize peer-reviewed academic journals that are written by experts and reviewed by other professionals in the field. This type of literature ensures that the research has been conducted with a certain amount of rigor, and the ideas presented are of acceptable quality (Laubepin, 2013). Instructors should show students how to examine the publication to see if it is peer reviewed by locating the journal for which the article was published in and determining whether that periodical utilizes the peer-review process (Library Guides, n.d.).

Once students have been taught the differences between the various sources, instructors should direct students in locating the literature both in print form and online. While there is much literature in print form, the rise of technology throughout the past several decades has made most scholarly work available exclusively online. Students will most likely go to Google or Google Scholar first to find peer-reviewed journal articles. Google can be a great source for information, however this should not be an end-all-be-all source. Much of what is presented on Google and Google Scholar is not considered a "scholarly source," but rather "popular literature" (Staines, Johnson, & Bonacci, 2008). Students will need to remember how to examine the publication to determine whether the information has been peer reviewed.

Most peer-reviewed journals are still primarily accessed through subscription-based databases, and university libraries are a great resource for students to be able to find this information. Most university libraries use EBSCO or JSTOR databases that provide students with access to a variety of scholarly sources. Searching through the web portal on the university library website is an easy and available way for students to find appropriate peer-reviewed journal articles. Students can search the online catalog, access information on the library's many collections, search online databases, and retrieve information in electronic formats (Staines et al., 2008). University libraries also have online forums where students can talk directly with a librarian and gain assistance in searching for information. Once on the library's website, students can very easily start finding credible articles by searching "key words" (e.g., "hot spot policing" and "crime") related to the topic at hand. Students can also narrow their searches by checking the box on the left labeled "peer-reviewed sources only."

For those peer-reviewed journal articles that are not freely available in full text through the library website, students can utilize the Interlibrary Loan Service. Students can use this free service to obtain books and articles, usually by filling out a form online with their name, school ID number, and email address. Libraries throughout the country loan other libraries the requested material for a given period of time. Students will receive an email that provides them with an electronic copy of the book or journal article that was requested. This opens up the opportunity for students to utilize an array of information and sources both in print and online.

Techniques to Help Students Read and Understand Scholarly Articles

Once students have been taught how to properly locate and identify peer-reviewed journal articles, they will need to be able to effectively read and understand the material that is presented within them. Scholarly journal articles are quite different than regular textbooks that are used in most college courses because they are essentially written for professional scientists (Bazerman, 1988). These types of articles contain new terminology, ideas, methods, and analyses that most students have not encountered before (Muench, 2000). Furthermore, journal articles typically have a standardized format that reads much differently from the popular literature that students are used to engaging with (Laubepin, 2013). Because most college students have never been taught how to properly read a journal article, they often struggle with the material when it is presented to them. Instead of reading through the entire article, students will pull material that is quoted from the abstract, tables, or opening paragraphs of the article (Emmons et al., 2010). Students then do not have the capacity to analyze and construct academic critiques (Ackerman & Arbour, 2016; Gillen, 2006). Therefore, it is critical for instructors to provide students with techniques in reading and understanding peer-reviewed journal articles.

Before students begin reading the article, instructors can provide cues to direct their reading. Using a template and requiring students to take notes while they read, advice can be given on main themes and theories to pay attention to that will help students focus while they read and avoid becoming overwhelmed with the content (McCrudden & Schraw, 2010). Additionally, having students take notes on the provided template will ultimately improve recall and comprehension (Purugganan & Hewitt, 2004).

TEMPLATE FOR TAKING NOTES ON PEER-REVIEWED JOURNAL ARTICLES

1. What is the problem being addressed?
2. What is the main theory(s) presented?
3. Discuss any previous research that has been conducted on the topic. What were the findings? What were the limitations?
4. Hypotheses or research questions:
5. Unit of analysis:
6. Independent and dependent variables:
7. Describe how the researchers collected their sample.
8. Describe the research design used.
9. Summarize the results of the study. What is *your* interpretation of the results?

10. Discussion/Conclusion: What was the authors' interpretation of the results? Do they match your interpretation? Do the findings agree/disagree with other literature on the topic? What are the limitations? Future directions?

Once students begin reading the article, they should be instructed to read the abstract and introduction first and identify the problem that is being addressed in the study (Purugganan & Hewitt, 2004; Raff, 2017). Next, students should read through the literature review and provide a summary of the background, including theoretical perspectives, previous work that has been conducted on the topic, limitations of prior research, and what the current authors will do to address those limitations (Raff, 2017). The methodology and results sections of an article may be the most difficult for students to read and comprehend, so it is important that instructors provide the most guidance during these sections. Requiring students to identify the hypotheses or research questions, as well as the unit of analysis and independent and dependent variables will provide them with an overarching look at the relationship being examined. From there, students should look for the procedures that are being used to conduct the research, including how subjects are sampled and what research designs are being employed (Purugganan & Hewitt, 2004; Raff, 2017). Students can reflect back on the material they learned in class or in their course textbook to recognize how that content is being utilized in real-life settings. In the results section, students should identify the results of the study and whether those findings were reported as significant or not (Gillen, 2006). Before moving on to the discussion and conclusion sections, students should attempt to provide their own interpretation of the results (Raff, 2017; Smith, 2001). This will give students practice in analyzing and developing academic critiques, and it encourages scientific thinking (Ackerman & Arbour, 2016; Gillen, 2006). Once students begin reading the discussion and conclusion sections, they should identify the conclusions related to the hypotheses, as well as the authors' interpretations of the results. Students should reflect how *their* interpretations of the results either support or contradict the *authors'* interpretations. Further, students should relay how the results either agree or disagree with prior research on the topic, limitations of the current research, and future directions that are suggested (Gillen, 2006; Purugganan & Hewitt, 2004;

Raff, 2017). Guiding students through this process in a systematic manner by focusing on the main themes of the article will allow students to better comprehend the material that is presented. Utilizing a template when reading these articles will also help students understand what to concentrate on, and ultimately act as a guiding system when reading peer-reviewed journal articles in the future.

Assessing Students' Understanding of the Material

Instructing students on how to properly identify and read a peer-reviewed journal article is important in courses related to research methods. This allows students to connect the terminology, ideas, and methods learned in class with research that is conducted in real-life settings. Yet, it is imperative that instructors assess whether students are understanding the material presented in scholarly journal articles so they can learn from their mistakes and better develop scientific thinking. One way to assess students' understanding of the material is to examine their responses on the template that was discussed in the previous section. After students have read through the article and written down their answers, instructors should collect their responses and provide individual feedback. Not only does this permit the instructor to gauge students' understanding of the material, but it provides students with feedback in areas where they may have struggled. It may also be beneficial to engage in a class discussion on areas where students as a whole may have struggled with grasping the material.

Another great way to assess students' comprehension of peer-reviewed journal articles is to utilize small group work. As we learned in Chapter 4, encouraging collaboration among learners through small group work is a great way to promote deep learning for students (Finlay & Faulkner, 2010). Fujimoto and colleagues (2011) found this in their study, where students shared that they appreciated small group work because it not only validated the views of the students, but it also helped to increase their understanding of the material. To accomplish this, students should first complete the reading and template on their own, and afterwards, small groups can be formed during class to discuss their answers. This will ensure that all students have read the material and completed the exercise, rather than only a select few of the group participants. Once in the groups, students are able to share their answers and interpretations of the findings related to the research. This will require them to explain their thinking process, discuss areas of agreement or disagreement, and cooperate to identify solutions to any disagreements (Finlay & Faulkner, 2010). Listening to and understanding different perspectives is also great practice for the collaboration that will be necessary when they begin their intended careers (Herrington, Oliver, & Reeves, 2003; Lave & Wenger, 1991). When groups are finished, the instructor should ask students to share their answers with the whole class. This permits the instructor instant feedback on students' comprehension and students the opportunity to hear perspectives from other groups.

Summary

It is likely that students who take a course in research methods will be required to engage with peer-reviewed journal articles. As we have discovered though, working with this material can be extremely challenging for students because they have either never had to read a journal article before or have never been properly taught how to navigate through an article. Students will find it extremely challenging then when they are required to utilize these articles to complete an exercise or assignment, and will instead pull out material from the abstract or tables (Emmons et al., 2010; Gillen, 2006). To promote deeper learning and the ability to form academic arguments, it is important that instructors take the time to guide students through locating and recognizing appropriate scholarly articles, as well as provide techniques for reading and understanding the material. Incorporating the recommendations presented in this chapter will better help students connect the terminology, ideas, and methods discussed in class to criminal justice research that is conducted in real-life settings. Using these suggestions in relation to scholarly journal articles will also promote active learning, higher-level thinking, and the ability to analyze and form credible arguments that can be advantageous for students once they enter into their intended careers (Ackerman & Arbour, 2016; Gillen, 2006).

References

Ackerman, E., & Arbour, B. K. (2016). "I have ten peer reviewed articles. Now what?" How political science research methods textbooks teach students about scholarly context. *The Journal of Academic Leadership, 42,* 612–619.

American Psychological Association. (n.d.). What are scientific journals? Retrieved February 15, 2018, from http://www.apa.org/advocacy/research/defending-research/scientific-journals.aspx

Bazerman, C. (1988). *Shaping written knowledge: The genre and activity of the experimental article in science.* Madison: University of Wisconsin Press.

Biggs, J. (1999). *Teaching for quality learning at university.* Buckingham, UK: Open University.

Cowie, B. (2012a, January 9). Part 2: Can first-year undergraduate students read primary scientific literature? [Blog post]. Retrieved from https://snowandscience.wordpress.com/2012/01/09/part-2-can-first-year-undergraduates-read-primary-scientific-literature/

Cowie, B. (2012b, February 10). Part 3: Can undergraduate students read primary scientific research articles? [Blog post]. Retrieved from https://snowandscience.wordpress.com/2012/02/10/part-3-can-undergraduate-students-read-primary-scientific-research-articles/

Emmons, M., Martin, W., Botts, C., & Amundson, C. (2010). Engaging sources: Information literacy and the freshman research paper (Part II). *LOEX Quarterly, 37*(2), 8–10.

Finlay, S., & Faulkner, G. (2010). Tête à tête: Reading groups and peer learning. *Active Learning in Higher Education, 6,* 32–45.

Fujimoto, Y., Hagel, P., Turner, P., Kattiyapornpong, U., & Zutshi, A. (2011). Helping university students to 'read' scholarly articles: The benefits of a structured and collaborative approach. *Journal of University Teaching & Learning Practice, 8*(3), 1–12.

Gillen, C. M. (2006). Criticism and interpretation: Teaching the persuasive aspects of research articles. *CBE Life Sciences Education, 5,* 34–8.

Herrington, J., Oliver, R., & Reeves, T. C. (2003). Patterns of engagement in authentic online learning environments. *Australian Journal of Educational Technology, 19*(1), 59–71.

Homel, R., Tomsen, S., & Thommeny, J. (1992). Public drinking and violence: Not just an alcohol problem. *The Journal of Drug Issues, 22*(3), 679–697.

Laubepin, F. (2013). *How to read (and understand) a social science journal article.* Ann Arbor, MI: Inter-university Consortium for Political and Social Research.

Lave, J., & Wenger, E. (1991). *Situated learning: Legitimate peripheral participation.* New York, NY: Cambridge University Press.

Library Guides. (n.d.). How to recognize peer-reviewed (refereed) journals. Retrieved February 15, 2018, from http://www.angelo.edu/services/library/handouts/peerrev.php

MacMillan, M., & MacKenzie, A. (2012). Strategies for integrating information literacy and academic literacy: Helping undergraduate students make the most of scholarly articles. *Library Management, 33*(8/9), 525–535.

McCrudden, M. T., & Schraw, G. (2010). The effects of relevance instructions and verbal ability on text processing. *Journal of Experimental Education, 78*, 96–117.

Muench, S. B. (2000). Choosing primary literature in biology to achieve specific educational goals. *Journal of College Science Teaching, 29*, 255–260.

Purugganan, M., & Hewitt, J. (2004). How to read a scientific article. Houston, TX: Rice University, Cain Project for Engineering and Professional Communication.

Rachal, K. C., Daigle, S., & Rachal, W. S. (2007). Learning problems reported by college students: Are they using learning strategies? *Journal of Instructional Psychology, 34*(4), 191–199.

Raff, J. (2017, December 6). How to read and understand a scientific paper: A step-by-step guide for non-scientists. *Huffpost*. Retrieved from https://www.huffingtonpost.com/jennifer-raff/how-to-read-and-understand-a-scientific-paper_b_5501628.html

Smith, G. R. (2001). Guided literature explorations. *Journal of College Science Teaching, 30*, 465–469.

Staines, G. M., Johnson, K., & Bonacci, M. (2008). *Social sciences research: Research, writing, and presentation strategies for students* (2nd ed.). Lanham, MD: Scarecrow Press.

Wright, R., Decker, S. H., Redfern, A. K., & Smith, D. L. (1992). A snowball's chance in hell: Doing fieldwork with active residential burglars. *Journal of Research in Crime and Delinquency, 29*(2), 148–161.

CHAPTER 6

Teaching APA Referencing Style in Research Methods

KEY CONCEPTS IN THE CHAPTER:

- Importance of teaching APA
- Best practices in teaching APA
- Topics to cover in APA instruction
- Examples and tips

We present an argument for the importance of teaching students a proper referencing style as part of their research methods courses. Our argument centers on the American Psychological Association (APA) style, despite the fact that many other suitable referencing styles would serve the same purpose. In fact, many students will begin college with little or no exposure to APA, having been taught MLA in high school. Regardless, we limit this chapter to APA for a few reasons. First, and most important, we selected APA because it is the most widely used citation source in criminal justice and criminology research. In addition, it is the dominate style in other closely related behavioral and social science fields such as psychology, counseling, and public health (American Psychological Association, 2010). The second reason is closely tied to the first. Because APA is so widely popular in criminal justice and criminology research, most of the articles students read will utilize APA. This allows for consistency across their reading and writing and will hopefully make proper APA referencing easier to master. Lastly, APA presents the dates of resources in-text unlike some other citation styles. This is important in criminal justice as ideas have evolved over previous decades, and the criminal justice system itself has changed. Different eras also have set the tone for the popularity of different criminological theories and research (e.g., popularity of labeling and Marxist theories in the 1960s and 1970s and the general theory of crime that emphasized internal causes of crime in the 1980s). It is for these for reasons that we chose to focus on APA referencing style.

The Importance of Teaching APA

Many of us have had the experience of grading papers when we suddenly read a passage that stands in stark contrast to the rest of the student's writing. A quick Google search reveals that the words are in fact not those of the student, but were copied from another's work. If you have not yet had this experience, you likely will before the end of your career as an instructor. Plagiarism is a widespread problem that has become even more prevalent with the Internet. In fact, research has found that academic misconduct has increased significantly over the past several years (McCabe, Trevino, & Butterfield, 2001), with plagiarism being one of the most common forms of academic dishonesty. The availability of large amounts of information has made it easier for students to plagiarize. Even the first lady, Melania Trump, was accused of plagiarizing her speech at the Republican National Convention from the former first lady, Michelle Obama (Allen, 2016). Electronic developments have also made it easier for instructors to detect plagiarism. It is increasingly important, therefore, that students learn proper citations and the importance of proper citations to avoid plagiarism. For students in criminal justice, this is especially important as a record of academic misconduct could impede their future career goals.

Ferree and Pfeifer (2011) discuss different levels of severity in plagiarism. They rate cutting and pasting passages as the most serious form of plagiarism, and not providing correct citations as the least serious form. Copying a few sentences or passages is considered to be in the middle of the severity spectrum. Although teaching proper citation will most likely only eliminate these "less serious" forms of plagiarism, it is arguably one of the most important types of plagiarism to prevent as more students who engage in this type of plagiarism do so without the intent of engaging in misconduct. Despite intent, however, they are often subjected to the same punishments and can suffer similar consequences to those who engage in the more serious forms of plagiarism with the intent of engaging in academic misconduct.

Research has found that students are often unable to correctly identify plagiarism and often engage in it because they do not realize they are plagiarizing or they do not perceive their actions as problematic (Marshall & Garry, 2005). Most of us have antidotal stories that support these findings. When discussing issues with plagiarism in their papers, we have often had students tell us that they did not realize they were plagiarizing. At many universities, students are responsible for reading and understanding the code of academic misconduct; however, detailed instruction on what is considered academic misconduct are not provided. Students are expected to recognize plagiarism and know how to avoid it. Making the issue more complicated, some instructors do not uphold the code by not requiring proper citation style. Therefore, students are suddenly made aware of their misconduct when an instructor enforces the standard even though they might have engaged in the same activities in another class and not have been reprimanded. By incorporating lessons on proper APA referencing, students can develop an understanding of plagiarism and avoid it by knowing when and how to properly cite sources.

Teaching APA to Criminal Justice Students

Requiring students to properly reference material in their papers can be especially important in criminal justice. Many students who major in criminal justice, and even those who choose to take a criminal justice course as an elective, often have very strong opinions about criminal justice issues.

In fact, it is often these strong opinions that sparked their interest in studying criminal justice. The advantage of this is that criminal justice students tend to be very passionate about the topics they study. The downside, however, is that their opinions are sometimes shaped by common myths, fictional media, literature portrayals of criminal justice issues, and by anecdotal evidence that is contrary to actual themes and patterns. These opinions can be so strong in criminal justice that when grading question responses, papers, and assignments instructors will find that students deviate from the readings and literature, instead offering long diatribes about what they believe to be true. When opinions are strong, students sometimes refuse to accept facts and valid research findings if they contradict their personal opinions. This presents a challenge for instructors as they try to produce graduates who can communicate and apply factual information once they enter into their careers. Requiring proper citations forces students to find real statistics and scientific literature to support their ideas. If they are unable to locate legitimate sources and provide citations of those sources, it can help them realize that what they believe to be true is not actually observed in the real world. Students who are able to move beyond their personal opinions will do better in their coursework and be better prepared for careers in criminal justice, especially careers in leadership positions. Even if they do not use APA in their jobs after college, learning to do so will hopefully cause them to take pause and consider whether their statements are defendable with independent and objective information, or if they are statements of pure opinion.

Another distinction regarding the importance of teaching criminal justice students APA referencing is teaching them to pay attention to detail when writing. On their jobs, many of them will have to complete official paperwork that is viewed and replied upon by several individuals. Mistakes on some of these documents could have major legal and ethical ramifications. In addition, some students will move into professions that require grant writing. With grants it is common for funding agencies to require submissions to follow specific formatting guidelines in order for applications to be reviewed. Students who are cognizant of these details will fare better with these tasks. Although these materials will not typically utilize APA, learning correct APA referencing will help students develop skills to pay attention to details in writing.

Best Practices in Teaching APA

APA instruction can be taught through instruction, or programs can require students to self-teach APA referencing. With the latter, instructors can simply assign the APA manual as a course textbook (or even simply recommended it) or another APA citation information tool. Instructors then place the burden on students to ensure they are properly utilizing and applying those resources. This is advantageous because it does not occupy class time. Research, however, has demonstrated that this is not the most effective approach. Instead, structured instruction results in greater student competence in APA referencing.

Luttrell, Bufkin, Eastman, and Miller (2010) evaluated the results of implementing a scientific writing class at Drury University to determine whether requiring students to learn APA referencing independently was as effective as including APA referencing in structured instruction. The course, titled Scientific Writing, was a one-credit requirement for all undergraduate students majoring in criminology, psychology, and sociology. It was designed to be a prerequisite to other research and statistics courses. In addition to teaching proper APA referencing, the course taught other formatting and stylistic best practices in scientific writing.

The course was assessed using a quasi-experimental design in which students who completed the Scientific Writing course were compared to a comparison group of upper-level students who did not take the course because it was not required when they began their programs. Students in both groups were administered a multiple-choice questionnaire before and after the course, and their performances were compared to determine their knowledge of APA referencing. Literature reviews written by all the students in the two groups also were compared. The results found that students who took the Scientific Writing course had statistically significant higher competencies in APA than students who did not take the course, illustrating the importance of teaching APA through structured instruction. In addition, the evaluation found no differences in quality of the literature reviews, despite the fact that the comparison group students were further along in their academic programs. Jorgensen and Marek (2013) similarly found that students who attended a workshop on APA referencing were more proficient in APA and better able to identify citation errors than those who did not attend a workshop.

Additional research finds that while students who receive structured instruction on APA referencing do better than those who are given resources to utilize to self-teach themselves referencing, students do even better if they are provided with both. Research has found that it is useful for students to learn the rules of APA through lecture and to subsequently have the opportunity to apply those rules independently (see Mandernach, Zafonte, & Taylor, 2016). Therefore, it will be most beneficial to students if instructors spend some class time lecturing on APA referencing as well as provide supplementary materials in which students practice referencing on their own. This can be done as in-class activities or homework assignments.

STUDENT ACTIVITY

Find a short research article, preferably one that is assigned in the class for another purpose. Assign the article to all students to read. Next, develop scenarios in which citations are presented from the article. Some should be correct APA referencing and some should be incorrect. Present an example of paraphrases and examples when ideas are presented but not cited. Examples of common mistakes can be illustrated as:

- Incorrect in-text citations
- Direct quote cited but not properly referenced
- Citations of original work copied and then cited as if they were original in the resource
- Paraphrasing
- Wording and sentence structure is different but ideas are copied without being cited
- Author names without dates
- List of authors not comprehensive
- Incorrect uses of "et al."
- Incorrect references

This assignment will be slightly time consuming but can be used semester after semester; tweaks will only be necessary if APA makes revisions to their referencing style. Additional examples can be added as the assignment is used more often. This assignment will also help identify which areas students are struggling in and prompt additional in-class instruction in that area.

Franz and Spitzer (2006) compared the effectiveness of teaching students APA with a template or a checklist. The template was an eight-page sample paper to serve as a model that students could reference when writing their own papers. The checklist served as a system for students to check their referencing. Pre- and posttests were compared for students who received classroom instruction that utilized a template only, a checklist only, and students who received classroom instruction that utilized both the template and the checklist. The results indicated that all three methods helped students learn APA. The template, however, was slightly more effective than the checklist despite students' comments complaining that it was boring. When the effectiveness of both was examined, the study found that using both resulted in the greatest increase in students' mastery of APA referencing. Given these findings, instructors should try to supply students with as many APA referencing resources as possible.

HELPFUL APA RESOURCES FOR INSTRUCTORS AND STUDENTS

https://owl.english.purdue.edu/owl/section/2/10/
https://www.library.kent.edu/files/APA_style.ppt
http://libguides.bgsu.edu/c.php?g=227185&p=1507882
http://blog.apastyle.org
https://www.lib.jjay.cuny.edu/research/apastyle1.pdf

While research has indicated that classroom instruction is an important part of students' mastery of APA, it is important for instructors to remember the dryness of the material. It is likely that one of the reasons why alternatives for teaching APA have been investigated in the literature is because instructors would prefer not to spend class time on APA. Given the technical nature of teaching APA, it should be expected to be less interesting to students. Therefore, it is important that instructors engage in active learning techniques. While the standard guideline is 15 minutes of lecture (see Wankat, 2002), when teaching APA referencing instructors might want to try to lecture for 10-minute intervals, incorporating more active learning assignments into the content. This can include individual and group work.

While teaching APA referencing, Mandernach and colleagues (2016) additionally recommend employing techniques in which students are asked to identify what they know, what they would like to know, and what they have learned (KWLs). They argue that this will help to identify areas in which students are struggling and need more assistance.

GROUP AND INDIVIDUAL STUDENT ACTIVITY

With this activity, you will need to have the same number of resources as 50% the number of students in your class. For example, if you have a class of 30, find 15 resources. Provide each student with one resource, yet have each resource assigned to two students. Ask the students to independently write the correct citation for their assigned resource. Once each student is finished, have the students find the other student with the same resource. Direct the students to compare the citations they wrote and discuss any discrepancies. After meeting with their partner, give them the opportunity to revise their citation before submitting it for grading. You can do this multiple times for each type of resource you use (e.g., book, journal article, website, newspaper, government report, personal communication, etc.). You might consider having students do multiple of the same type of resource (e.g., book, article, and website) but with a different number of authors or no author.

Traditional quizzes are also a useful tool to determine students' mastery of APA referencing and to identify areas in which students need additional guidance. Quizzes can be administered during class or online. During quizzes, the best test of knowledge would be garnered by allowing students to use their notes and references. Knowing where to find correct APA referencing information, and taking the time to look up that information when writing a paper or assignment, is true mastery of APA referencing.

EXAMPLE QUIZ QUESTIONS

1. **The words "Running Head" should appear:**
    a) On the top of every page
    b) On the bottom of every page
    c) On the top of the title page only
    d) On the bottom of the title page only

2. **APA papers should be:**
    a) Double spaced
    b) Single spaced
    c) Double or single spaced as long as it is consistent throughout the paper

3. **Page numbers should be included in the in-text citation when:**
    a) An author's research findings are summarized
    b) Using a direct quote
    c) An author's ideas are summarized
    d) All of the above

4. **In-text citations should always include:**
    a) Author last name and year of publication
    b) Author last name, year of publication, and title of the reference
    c) Author *first and last* name, year of publication, and title of the reference
    d) Author last name, year of publication, title of the reference, and page number

5. **Which journal article reference is correct?**
    a) Merton, R. K. (1938). Social structure and anomie. American Sociological Review, 3(5), 672–682.
    b) Merton, R. K. (1938). Social structure and anomie. *American Sociological Review, 3*(5), 672–682.
    c) Merton, Robert K. (1938). Social structure and anomie. *American Sociological Review, 3*(5), 672–682.
    d) Merton, R. K. (1938). Social structure and anomie. American Sociological Review, 3(5), pages 672–682.

6. **Which book reference is correct?**
   a) Gottfredson, M. R., & Hirschi, T. (1990). *A General Theory of Crime.* Stanford, CA: Stanford University Press.
   b) Gottfredson, Michael R., & Hirschi, Travis (1990). *A general theory of crime.* Stanford, CA: Stanford University Press.
   c) Gottfredson, Michael R., & Hirschi, Travis (1990). *A General Theory of Crime.* Stanford, CA: Stanford University Press.
   d) Gottfredson, M. R., & Hirschi, T. (1990). *A general theory of crime.* Stanford, CA: Stanford University Press.

7. **When citing a website with no date, which in-text citation is correct?**
   a) (U.S. Census)
   b) (U.S. Census, date not available)
   c) (U.S. Census, n.d.)
   d) (U.S. Census, date)

8. **Which in-text citation is correct?**
   a) According to (Merton 1938)....
   b) According to Merton (1938)...
   c) According to Merton 1938...
   d) According to *Merton 1938...*

9. **On the reference page, references should be organized:**
   a) by number of authors, with sources with more authors listed first
   b) alphabetically
   c) by date, with newest references first
   d) by date, with oldest references first

Answers: c, a, b, a, c, d, c, b, b

What Should APA Instruction Include?

Research conducted by Mandernach et al. (2016) identified specific APA concepts with which students commonly have the most difficulty. They collected a random sample of student research papers that had already been graded to determine common themes in APA errors. These errors were then presented to faculty, and the faculty were asked to rate how often they encountered those errors in their students' writing on a scale from "never" to "frequently." The results indicated that students had the most difficulty with the formatting of and use of in-text citations and formatting of references on the reference page, with over half of faculty indicating that they encountered these problems in students' papers frequently. Over 40% of faculty also frequently found issues with using direct quotes and the proper formatting of direct quoting. About a third of faculty also frequently found problems with the proper use of headings and subheadings. Given these findings, we recommend that instructors focus heavily on these three concepts.

INSTRUCTOR TIP

Students will further benefit if all instructors in your department require and use APA. Handouts, assignments, essays, etc. that instructors distribute to students should follow APA guidelines. This demonstrates the importance of professionalism in writing and reinforces the mechanics of APA referencing. If instructors are not practicing professional writing, it sends the message to students that it is not important and that a sloppy display of information is acceptable.

Grading Tips

When students submit written work, be sure to include APA assessments on the grading rubric. Break it down to points awarded for proper in-text citations, proper referencing, displaying quotes correctly, using correct headings and subheadings, title page, abstract, organization of paper, etc. Be sure to provide a copy of the rubric to students prior to them starting their papers. This will communicate the importance of proper referencing.

Feedback also is important; however, detailed feedback when grading the correct use of APA referencing can be time consuming for the instructor. Mandernach et al. (2016) recommend that instructors make detailed comments and corrections to assignments, and then allow students to go back to assignments that have been graded and fix the errors they made for full or partial credit. Correcting each error can fail pedagogically, however, as students simply rush through the changes the professor essentially did for them—especially if track changes in Word is used and students can simply accept the corrections. A better learning technique would be for students to self-identify errors and correct them for partial credit. Instructors can highlight citations and references that are incorrect and leave it up to the student to identify the specific error (Mandernach et al., 2016). If a student makes the same mistake on several references, the instructor should correct one incident and direct the student to look over the others carefully to identify and make the corrections. If a mistake is common across many students in a class, the instructor should also consider addressing the issue with the entire class and challenging the students to identify whether they made those mistakes. Students will then be responsible for determining what needs to be corrected based on the instructor's additional lesson. Another way instructors can reduce their grading burden is to follow Mandernach et al.'s (2016) suggestion by having students conduct peer reviews of fellow students' papers for APA errors. Students should then be given the opportunity to correct errors their peers identified. This should reduce the number of errors prior to the instructor grading the assignment.

Summary

Students accrue many benefits by learning correct APA referencing style during their research methods courses. This is especially true for criminal justice students, some of whom will be in careers in which their written documents will be heavily scrutinized or whose tasks will involve detail-oriented writing. Teaching APA can also prevent cases of plagiarism in which students are unaware that they need to properly cite information. Several studies have indicated that APA referencing is best taught through in-class structured instruction paired with resources and other applied learning techniques. Furthermore, it is important that all instructors in a department remain consistent in their use and enforcement of proper APA referencing in students' work. During instruction, instructors should be sure to focus on in-text citations, references, and direct quotes, as students frequently have issues with these topics. To enforce the importance of proper APA referencing, instructors also must assign a portion of a student's grade to proper APA referencing, provide feedback to students making APA mistakes, and provide students the opportunity to correct their mistakes so they learn to use APA referencing correctly going forward.

References

Allen, C. (2016, July 19). Was Melania Trump's speech plagiarized from Michelle Obama? USA Politics. Retrieved from https://www.usatoday.com/story/news/politics/onpolitics/2016/07/19/melania-trump-republican-convention-speech-plagiarism/87278088/

American Psychological Association. (2010). *Publication manual of the American Psychological Association* (6th ed.). Washington, DC: Author.

Dawson, M. M., & Overfield, J. A. (2006). Plagiarism: Do students know what it is? *Bioscience Education, 8*(1), 1–15.

Ferree, C. W., & Pfeifer, H. L. (2011). The 'write' stuff: Simple techniques designed to teach students how to avoid plagiarism. *Journal of Criminal Justice Education, 22*(2), 286–303.

Franz, T. M., & Spitzer, T. M. (2006). Different approaches to teaching the mechanics of American Psychological Association style. *Journal of Scholarship of Teaching and Learning, 6*(2), 13–20.

Jorgensen, T. D., & Marke, P. (2013). Workshops increase students' proficiency at identifying style writing errors. *Teaching Psychology, 40*(4), 259–267.

Luttrell, V. R., Bufkin, J. L., Eastman, V. J., & Miller, R. (2010). Teaching scientific writing: Measuring student learning in an intensive APA skills course. *Teaching of Psychology, 37*, 193–195.

Mandernach, B. J., Zafonte, M., & Taylor, C. (2016). Instructional strategies to improve college students' APA style writing. *International Journal of Teaching and Learning in Higher Education, 27*(3), 407–412.

Marshall, S., & Garry, M. (2005). How well do students really understand plagiarism? [Blog post]. Retrieved from http://www.ascilite.org/conferences/brisbane05/blogs/proceedings/52_Marshall.pdf

McCabe, D. L., Trevino, L. K., & Butterfield, K. D. (2001). Cheating in academic institutions: A decade of research. *Ethics & Behavior, 11*(3), 219–232.

Wankat, P. (2002). *The effective efficient professor: Teaching, scholarship and service.* Boston, MA: Allyn and Bacon.

CHAPTER 7

Assessing Student Learning

KEY CONCEPTS IN THE CHAPTER:

- The importance of testing
- Quizzing: In-class and online
- Traditional versus performance-based assessment
- Utilizing textbook or publisher-supplied assessment tools

As instructors in research methods courses, we strive to integrate active learning techniques into the classroom to enhance the learning process and encourage long-term retention. However, when we assess student learning through quizzes and examinations we tend to rely on methods that require students to memorize concepts rather than engage in higher-level thinking (Connor-Greene, 2000). It is important to understand why testing is so important to the learning process, and the various forms of assessment that are available that will allow instructors to tap into different knowledge bases. Frequent testing can significantly improve students' performances on subsequent exams, as well as promote long-term retention even after the course concludes (Roediger, Putnam, & Smith, 2011; Carpenter, Pashler, Wixted, & Vul, 2008). Instructors can implement various forms of quizzing that will improve the likelihood that students complete assigned readings, increase their participation in class discussions, and improve their performance on subsequent exams. Moreover, various forms of assessment exist with regards to testing that instructors can create. Traditional forms of assessment, as well as performance-based assessments, allow instructors to accomplish several objectives that will gauge students' understanding of course content. Not only can instructors identify whether students are able to recall information presented during class instruction, but they can measure students' abilities to apply complex thinking to real-world examples (Educational Testing Service, 2003; Frederiksen, 1984; Frey & Schmitt, 2007; Reeves, 2000).

The Importance of Testing

We often think of testing in higher education simply as an evaluation tool for assessing students and assigning them grades (Roediger & Karpicke, 2006). However, testing serves a far greater purpose and plays a critical role in fostering student learning. As much of prior literature suggests, the use of testing (e.g., quizzes or examinations) improves student performance because of the active retrieval of information that occurs during the testing process. Known as the "testing effect," this retrieval process makes course material more memorable and encourages long-term retention of the information (Carpenter, 2012; Carpenter & Kelly, 2012; Roediger & Karpicke, 2006). Many scholars have found support for this phenomenon, determining that students tend to retain information better if they have previously been tested on the content, compared to simply studying the information or having no practice at all (Carpenter et al., 2008; Nungester & Duchastel, 1982; Roediger et al., 2011).

Indirect effects of testing have also been offered throughout much of the literature and warrant mention here. The use of testing affords both students and instructors the opportunity to identify gaps in students' knowledge. Results or feedback from a test can determine areas where students excelled in the course content, as well as identify areas of weakness (Roediger & Karpicke, 2006; Roediger et al., 2011). Students can then go back to their course materials and review the information for which they did not know the correct answers. Moreover, feedback provides insight for instructors on areas where students struggled with certain course material. Instructors can then work with students to review that material again and potentially offer additional exercises to practice the application of those concepts. This practice will ultimately help students perform better on subsequent exams and retain that information long-term. In fact, Rohrer, Taylor, and Sholar (2010) established that students who engaged in testing where feedback was provided to them performed significantly better on a subsequent exam than students who simply studied the material that was provided to them.

While instructors want to see their students perform well on course exams and quizzes, we also want students to be able to transfer the knowledge they learn in class to new situations. This skill becomes especially vital in research methods courses, where students are often required to apply various concepts, methods, and designs to real-world scenarios. The use of testing improves students' chances of being able to accomplish this feat. Retrieval practice through the use of testing encourages information that can be used to solve new problems (Roediger et al., 2011). For example, testing students through an exercise or quiz on the fundamental components and processes of quasi-experimental research designs will improve their ability to apply that information to a subsequent exam that covers similar content. Then, when students are instructed to design an experiment to test a given hypothesis (e.g., "probationers who have been ordered to be on electronic monitoring will have fewer rates of technical violations, compared to probationers who have not been ordered on electronic monitoring"), they will be able to retrieve the knowledge previously learned and apply it to a new context. Thinking even further down the road, students can transfer this knowledge to new situations they may encounter in their prospective careers.

It is evident that testing is an important component of college courses, especially in research-related courses; however, tests do not come without criticisms attached. Testing, through quizzes or examinations, requires a lot of effort on the instructor's part and implementing tests can take time away from class instruction (Educational Testing Service, 2003; Urtel, Bahamonde,

Mikesky, & Vessely, 2006). However, as discussed in Chapter 4, sometimes smaller doses of testing can be accomplished through the use of exercises or brief quizzes that will engage students and promote active learning. Additionally, instructors can decide the frequency or optimal spacing gap (Chapter 3) with which they implement different forms of testing. It has been noted that learning will continue to increase as the frequency of classroom testing increases. Nonetheless, Bangert-Drowns, Kulik, and Kulik (1991) did find that even administering just one test can produce greater gains in learning, compared to no tests at all.

Quizzing

Instructors may regularly find that students tend to come to class without having read the required readings. As such, students are unprepared, and this affects the overall classroom atmosphere (e.g., lower student involvement, lower quality discussions, etc.) (Marcell, 2008). This can be extremely detrimental to courses in research methods, as much of the material tends to be dense and requires multiple exposures to absorb the content. We know that learning expands when students are actively engaged in the course content (Angelo, 1995). One tool to help promote the learning process and avoid the issues presented is to implement regular quizzing. Research often finds that quizzing is associated with improved understanding of course material (Johnson & Kiviniemi, 2009; Marchant, 2002), increased class attendance (Wilder, Flood, & Stromsnes, 2001), and higher performance on exams (DeSouza & Fleming, 2003; McDaniel, Anderson, Derbish, & Morrisette, 2007). For example, Marcell (2008) found that courses which implemented regular quizzing had students who asked over twice as many reading-related questions and were significantly more prepared for class than courses that did not implement quizzes. When students are aware they will be quizzed on the course readings, it encourages them to complete the required readings, continuously study, participate more in class, understand course-related concepts better, and interact more with the instructor (Fitch, Drucker, & Norton, 1951; Johnson & Kiviniemi, 2009; Marcell, 2008; Roediger et al., 2011). In fact, several scholars have shared that even students tend to find regular quizzing helpful. Students have shared that quizzing helped them to determine areas of strengths and weaknesses related to knowledge of the material, they felt they absorbed the material better since they knew they would be tested on it, and the quizzes helped them to develop better study habits (Marcell, 2008; Urtel et al., 2006; White & Hammer, 2000).

In-Class Quizzes

One of the more traditional methods of implementing regular quizzes is in the form of in-class testing. Instructors can administer quizzes either at the beginning or end of the class period, where they can assess student knowledge on assigned readings, previous class content, or material that was taught in the current session. The idea of "regular quizzing" may seem overwhelming for many instructors. It is important to note that the term "regular" can be flexible. As discussed, learning improves as the frequency of testing increases; however, even implementing one assessment produces gains in learning (Bangert-Drowns et al., 1991). Thus, instructors can decide to implement a quiz as often as their course schedule allows. This may resemble a quiz in each class session, once per week, once every other week, and so on. Instructors can also decide on the amount of content to cover in each quiz. For instance, quizzes can be incorporated as a form of low-stakes assessments (Chapter 2) that are anywhere from one open-ended question that requires students to apply a concept to a given example to five multiple choice questions that test students' recognition of the assigned reading material. Additionally, the type of feedback that students receive can be selected in accordance to the instructor's preference. If the instructor administers the in-class quiz at the beginning of the session, it may be advantageous to discuss the answers as an entire class to act as a beginning point of discussion. Or, if time does not permit, the instructor may collect the quizzes and provide individual feedback. During the next class session the instructor can hand back the graded quizzes and either discuss general areas of weakness or advise students to discuss any areas of concern with the instructor outside of class time (Connor-Greene, 2000). While incorporating in-class quizzes can take away from class instruction, it is helpful for instructors to know that certain steps can be taken to reduce this potential burden (Urtel et al., 2006).

In-class quizzing presents several advantages to the learning process in higher education, including the increased probability that students will spend more time reading assigned course material outside of class (Fitch et al., 1951). They will feel more prepared for class sessions and assessments, as well as increase their participation in class discussions and questioning. Moreover, in-class quizzes incorporate daily writing into the course (Connor-Greene, 2000; Marcell, 2008). All of these benefits work together through the use of testing to ultimately maximize student learning and long-term retention.

Online Quizzes

While in-class quizzing presents an admirable method to consistently test students on course material and enhance their learning process, instructors may continue to find difficulties in incorporating in-class quizzes on a regular basis due to time constraints. With the advance of technology over the past several decades, most students now have access to the Internet and know how to effectively navigate through it. Likewise, it has become much easier for instructors to integrate online quizzing into the classroom. This method of quizzing provides much of the same benefits as in-class quizzes, with some added bonuses. Similar to in-class quizzes, online assessments motivate students to complete the assigned readings because they know they are going to be tested on the material (Johnson & Kiviniemi, 2009). By incorporating this, students will be prepared for subsequent class sessions, and will likely be more willing to participate in class discussions (Hillman, 2012). Moreover, online quizzes tend to be much easier for instructors to administer, as they can usually set up the quiz ahead of time and then select an activation and due date for the assessment (DeSouza & Fleming, 2003). These often can be created through the university's website or through an outside publisher source, which we will touch on later in the chapter. Once students complete the quiz, instant feedback can be administered that notifies students of any incorrect answers, allowing them the opportunity to learn from their mistakes and improve on subsequent assessments. Instructors can take this one step further by offering a general explanation for why an answer was deemed incorrect or provide cues on where to find the content in the textbook (Johnson & Kiviniemi, 2009).

Traditional Versus Performance-Based Assessment

As noted in previous chapters, there has been a substantial increase in the acceptance of and use of active learning methods in higher education. However, when it comes to testing, instructors still tend to use assessments that rely on memorization rather than higher-level thinking (Connor-Greene, 2000; King, 1995). A variety of testing forms exist, including multiple choice, true-false, matching, short answer, essay, and projects, among others. No single form of assessment works well in all situations and for all purposes, and each presents its' own strengths and weaknesses. Most instructors also know that some students tend to perform better on certain types of assessments, whereas some students excel at other forms (Educational Testing Service, 2003). The type or combination of assessments will likely depend on the nature of the information being taught, the purpose of the course instruction, and what the instructor wants to learn from the assessment (Educational Testing Service, 2003).

Traditional forms of assessment are generally the most popular types of testing in higher education courses, and include multiple choice, true-false, matching, and short answer. These tests tend to focus on memorization skills and direct students to identify or select the correct response to a given question or statement (Educational Testing Service, 2003). The advantage of using these forms of testing is that they can assess a broad scope of knowledge quickly. In addition, they can be simple and easy to administer and grade, especially for larger classes, and the amount of subjectivity is reduced with grading because there is a well-defined correct answer (Bailey, 1998; Educational Testing Service, 2003; Herbst, 1975; Law & Eckes, 1995). However, construction of the actual test may be more time consuming for instructors, and because students are provided a set of potential answers, it may be easier for them to guess and receive the correct answer (Cunningham, 1998; Educational Testing Service, 2003; Herbst, 1975; Simonson, Smaldino, Albright, & Zvacek, 2000). Furthermore, these forms of assessment generally test memory and recognition rather than complex, higher-level thinking. Nonetheless, some content in research methods courses may only warrant the purpose of recognition rather than applied abilities. For example, instructors want to learn whether students are able to recall information related to ethical standards in research. In this case, utilizing traditional forms of assessments are likely sufficient to test this knowledge base, and more extensive methods of assessment may not be necessary.

While traditional methods may be useful, instructors should still consider incorporating additional forms of assessment into their tests that will provide a more comprehensive picture of students' knowledge, abilities, and skills related to course content (Rudner & Boston, 1994; Wiggins, 1989). This can be extremely beneficial in research methods courses because much of the material learned acts as only a component to a much grander process. Students are taught material on units of analysis, variables, hypotheses, and research designs, among other topics, and then expected to piece that information together and apply it to a real-world scenario. This feat can be difficult for students to accomplish if they are not afforded the ability to work through examples and understand how the research process operates. To overcome this, performance assessments can be incorporated that involve students performing a task or demonstrating their work on several different knowledge bases to create a final product (Educational Testing Services, 2003; Office of Technology Assessment, 1992). Examples of performance assessments include open-ended questions, capstone projects, portfolios, or conducting research (Rudner & Boston, 1994). We have included several examples below of performance-based test questions that may be utilized in a research methods course.

POTENTIAL PERFORMANCE-BASED TEST QUESTIONS

(1) You are interested in comparing arrest records of substance-involved offenders with those offenders who do not use substances. From this information: (1) define a hypothesis, (2) create a nondirectional hypothesis, (3) create a directional hypothesis, and (4) explain which type of directional hypothesis you created.

(2) Design a classical experiment to test the following hypothesis: "Neighborhoods that have police officers patrolling on foot will have higher perceptions of safety compared to neighborhoods without foot patrols." Be sure to identify your independent and dependent variables, and explain how you will measure each.

You should also address each step that you will take to conduct the experiment, as well as identify and explain whether the criteria for causation have been met.

(3) As a researcher, you are interested in studying how newly incarcerated offenders adjust to prison life. Design a field study that will allow you to investigate this topic. Be sure to include all relevant details in your study design.

As you can see, the examples presented above require students to perform challenging tasks that involve multiple steps. These tasks evaluate students' problem-solving skills, their ability to transfer knowledge to real-world situations, and they assess multiple domains of course content at the same time (Educational Testing Service, 2003; Frederiksen, 1984; Frey & Schmitt, 2007; Reeves, 2000). As such, this form of assessment may be appealing to instructors in research methods courses considering the purpose of much instruction is to apply the concepts of research to real-life examples. The detail that is required in students' answers also gives instructors the opportunity to gauge whether students really understand the material, as well as specific areas where students may struggle (Rudner & Boston, 1994). Yet, these open-ended questions mean that grading becomes much more time consuming. Instructors must carefully read through each student's response and gauge whether the student has a sufficient understanding of course content. This also introduces a greater amount of subjectivity, considering there may be several ways to correctly answer a particular question (Educational Testing Service, 2003; Herbst, 1975).

It becomes evident as we move through this section that both traditional and performance-based assessments present many benefits and challenges to the testing process. So, which method lends itself superior to research-based courses? The decision remains with the instructor and depends on the nature of the information being taught, the purpose of the instruction, and what the instructor hopes to learn from the assessment (Educational Testing Service, 2003). Utilizing both forms of assessment within a single test may be a great option so that instructors can assess students' abilities to both recall information and critically think about certain content. Herbst (1975) supports this claim, stating that traditional methods should not be in competition with performance-based assessments, but rather complementary. Moreover, we know that students tend to excel at some forms of assessment over others. Incorporating more than one type of assessment within a test reduces the chances that students will be penalized simply because they tend to perform weaker on a given type of assessment.

Test Preparation

For whichever form of assessment is used, instructors should keep in mind several important objectives when preparing a quiz or test. Each item on a test should measure a course learning outcome, and should represent the concepts and skills that were previously emphasized during course instruction (Cohen & Wollack, 2006; Devine & Yaghlian, n.d.). Furthermore, directions for each test item should be clear and concise. Instructors should not assume that students will understand the directions, but instead should elaborate to students what is expected of them for a given question or task. If there is anything that may be considered confusing for students, instructors should make an additional effort to go through the directions as an entire class at the beginning of the testing period (Educational Testing Service, 2003). Furthermore, instructors need to keep time limits in mind when constructing any form of assessment. Tests should be designed so that students are able to complete the assessment in the allotted time frame. If not, students will either rush to finish the test or will not answer the questions at the end. As a result, instructors are not able to gauge students' knowledge and ability on these topics (Educational Testing Service, 2003). Finally, another important objective to keep in mind when preparing course assessments is to arrange test items in a way that makes the most sense. For example, tests should be organized so that all items of the same assessment type (e.g., multiple-choice, short answer, open-ended tasks, etc.) and subject matter are grouped together. It is also suggested that test items should be arranged in an order of increasing difficulty (Devine & Yaghlian, n.d.).

As we focus exclusively on different types of assessments, a few helpful tips can be offered for constructing multiple choice questions. When preparing these items, instructors should remember to use simple and clear language, as well as place most of the wording in the question or statement rather than the answer set (Burton, Sudweeks, Merrill, & Wood, 1991). Attempts should be implemented to avoid the use of negative wording;

however, if this is needed then instructors should emphasize the negative item by bolding or italicizing the word (Devine & Yaghlian, n.d.). Moreover, the intended answer for each item should be, above all, the clear and correct choice of the given answer set. Instructors would be wise to include common misconceptions and errors as additional answer choices to enhance the learning process (Cunningham, 1998; Devine & Yaghlian, n.d.).

When designing performance-based assessments, instructors should utilize four key objectives. First, instructors should identify the desired goals and objectives that need to be achieved through each task, as well as which skills students should be able to use to accomplish a given challenge. Second, criteria for each question need to be established that will determine the difficulty level for which students need to perform at. Third, specific directions need to be created that will offer students a clear understanding of what is expected of them in each task. Finally, instructors need to design a scoring method that will constitute which answers are deemed incorrect, acceptable, or outstanding (Rudner & Boston, 1994).

Utilizing Textbook or Publisher-Supplied Assessment Tools

Many course textbooks today now come with resources for both students and instructors, including instructor-edition books, computerized study guides and quizzes, supplemental readings, and curriculum development support, among others (Flora & Logan, 1996). Utilizing these tools allows students to become more engaged in the course content and better prepared for class; it also enhances their critical-thinking skills, and often provides instant feedback on areas they are struggling with (Brinkley et al., 1999). Luckily, with the advance of technology today, a multitude of services are out there that offer these benefits. McGraw-Hill Education is one such publisher that has become extremely popular within higher education. McGraw-Hill Education utilizes evidence-based research to engage students and instructors in the learning process (McGraw-Hill Higher Education, 2017). Instructors in the criminal justice field can browse course textbooks, participate in free online workshops about classroom strategies and the use of technology, and read through a variety of blogs that address general teaching approaches (McGraw-Hill Higher Education, 2017). More specifically, McGraw-Hill Education offers "Connect," which is a learning management system that allows instructors to integrate online content into their course. The assignments and quizzes provided engage students in course material and offer immediate grading and feedback. As we have learned, this feedback not only helps students identify strengths and weaknesses in their course knowledge, but it helps instructors gauge areas of concern in the material that may need further attention (McGraw-Hill Higher Education, 2017).

Additional popular companies that offer useful resources and assessment tools include Cengage, Pearson, and Wiley Education Services. Like McGraw-Hill, these publishers create a learning environment for both students and instructors that enhance their academic abilities with both in-class and online material (Cengage Learning, n.d.; Pearson, n.d.; Wiley Education Services, 2018). Instructors have the capabilities to browse by their respective discipline and find course textbooks, webinars, and digital resources to use within the course curriculum. The advantage is that much of these resources meet students where they are at in the learning process (Wiley Education Services, 2018). These interactive experiences allow students to expand their knowledge base, develop writing skills, and tackle challenges that will benefit them throughout the course, as well as in their perspective careers.

HELPFUL RESOURCES FOR INSTRUCTORS:

McGraw-Hill Higher Education: https://www.mheducation.com/highered/home-guest.html
Cengage: https://www.cengage.com/
Pearson: https://www.pearson.com/us/higher-education.html
Wiley Education Services: https://edservices.wiley.com/

Summary

Testing is a crucial component of the learning process, as it enhances students' abilities to understand course content and achieve long-term retention of the information (Roediger et al., 2011). This chapter has shown us that testing not only improves students' performances on subsequent exams, but it allows both students and instructors the opportunity to identify gaps in their knowledge base and improve their ability to transfer knowledge to new contexts (Roediger & Karpicke, 2006; Roediger et al., 2011). The inclusion of *frequent* quizzes or examinations further increases a students' learning capacity and can improve class participation (Bangert-Drowns et al., 1991). As we have discussed, instructors can utilize various forms of assessment to assess students' understanding of course content. Both traditional and performance-based assessments can identify whether students are able to recall information offered during course instruction, as well as measure a student's ability to apply concepts and processes to real-life examples (Educational Testing Service, 2003; Frederiksen, 1984; Frey & Schmitt, 2007; Reeves, 2000). Instructors can utilize this information, as well as additional textbook and publisher-supplied assessment tools, to decide which forms of assessment will work best for their teaching style and intended course objectives.

References

Angelo, T. A. (1995). Classroom assessment for critical thinking. *Teaching of Psychology, 22*, 6–7.

Bailey, K. M. (1998). *Learning about language assessment: Dilemmas, decisions, and directions.* Boston, MA: Heinle & Heinle.

Bangert-Drowns, R. L., Kulik, J. A., & Kulik, C. L. C. (1991). Effects of frequent classroom testing. *Journal of Educational Research, 85*, 89–99.

Brinkley, A., Dessants, B., Flamm, M., Fleming, C., Forcey, C., & Rothschild, E. (1999). The *Chicago handbook for teachers: A practice guide to the college classroom.* Chicago, IL: University of Chicago Press.

Burton, S. J., Sudweeks, R. R., Merrill, P. F., & Wood, B. (1991). *How to prepare better multiple-choice test items: Guidelines from university faculty.* Brigham Young University Testing Services, The Department of Instructional Science. Retrieved from https://testing.byu.edu/handbooks/betteritems.pdf

Carpenter, S. K. (2012). Testing enhances the transfer of learning. *Current Directions in Psychological Science, 21*(5), 279–283.

Carpenter, S. K., & Kelly, J. W. (2012). Tests enhance retention and transfer of spatial learning. *Psychonomic Bulletin Review, 19*, 443–448.

Carpenter, S. K., Pashler, H., Wixted, J. T., & Vul, E. (2008). The effects of tests on learning and forgetting. *Memory & Cognition, 36*, 438–448.

Cengage Learning. (n.d.). Retrieved May 1, 2018, from https://www.cengage.com

Cohen, A., & Wollack, J. (2006). *Handbook on test development: Helpful tips for creating reliable and valid classroom tests.* Madison: Testing & Evaluation Services, University of Wisconsin-Madison.

Connor-Greene, P. A. (2000). Assessing and promoting student learning: Blurring the line between teaching and testing. *Teaching of Psychology, 27*(2), 84–88.

Cunningham, G. K. (1998). *Assessment in the classroom: Constructing and interpreting texts.* Bristol, PA: Falmer Press, Taylor & Francis.

DeSouza, E., & Fleming, M. (2003). A comparison of in-class vs. online quizzes on student exam performance. *Journal of Computing in Higher Education, 14*, 121–134.

Devine, M., & Yaghlian, N. (n.d.). *Test construction manual: Construction of objective tests.* Ithaca, NY: Center for Teaching Innovation, Cornell University.

Educational Testing Service. (2003). Linking classroom assessment with student learning. Retrieved from https://www.ets.org/Media/Tests/TOEFL_Institutional_Testing_Program/ELLM2002.pdf

Fitch, M. L., Drucker, A. J., & Norton, J. A. (1951). Frequent testing as a motivating factor in large lecture courses. *Journal of Educational Psychology, 42*, 1–20.

Flora, S. R., & Logan, R. E. (1996). Using computerized study guides to increase performance on general psychology examinations: An experimental analysis. *Psychological Reports, 79*, 235–241.

Frederiksen, F. (1984). The real test bias: Influences of testing on teaching and learning. *American Psychologist, 39*(3), 193–202.

Frey, B. B., & Schmitt, V. L. (2007). Coming to terms with classroom assessment. *Journal of Advanced Academics, 18*(3), 402–423.

Herbst, L. J. (1975). Objective testing in higher education. *The Vocational Aspect of Education, 27*(66), 21–25.

Hillman, J. (2012). The impact of online quizzes on student engagement and learning. Retrieved from http://berks.psu.edu/sites/default/files/campus/Hillman_TLI_report.pdf

Johnson, B. C., & Kiviniemi, M. T. (2009). The effect of online chapter quizzes on exam performance in an undergraduate social psychology course. *Teaching of Psychology, 36*, 33–37.

King, A. (1995). Inquiring minds really do want to know: Using questioning to teach critical thinking. *Teaching of Psychology, 22*, 13–17.

Law, B., & Eckes, M. (1995). *Assessment and ESL.* Manitoba, Canada: Peguis Publishers.

Marcell, M. (2008). Effectiveness of regular online quizzing in increasing class participation and preparation. *International Journal for the Scholarship of Teaching and Learning, 2*(1), 1–9.

Marchant, G. J. (2002). Student reading of assigned articles: Will this be on the test? *Teaching of Psychology, 29*, 49–51.
McDaniel, M. A., Anderson, J. L., Derbish, M. H., & Morrisette, N. (2007). Testing the testing effect in the classroom. *European Journal of Cognitive Psychology, 19*, 494–513.
McGraw-Hill Higher Education. (2017). Retrieved May 1, 2018, from https://www.mheducation.com/highered/home-guest.html
Nungester, R. J., & Duchastel, P. C. (1982). Testing versus review: Effects on retention. *Journal of Educational Psychology, 74*, 18–22.
Office of Technology Assessment. (1992). *Testing in American schools: Asking the right questions.* Washington, DC: Government Printing Office.
Pearson. (n.d.). Retrieved May 1, 2018, from https://www.pearson.com/us/higher-education.html
Reeves, T. C. (2000). Alternative assessment approaches for online learning environments in higher education. *Educational Computing Research, 3*(1), 101–111.
Roediger, H. L., & Karpicke, J. D. (2006). The power of testing memory: Basic research and implications for educational practice. *Perspectives on Psychological Science, 1*(3), 181–210.
Roediger, H. L., Putnam, A. L., & Smith, M. A. (2011). The benefits of testing and their applications to educational practice. *Psychology of Learning and Motivation, 55*, 1–36.
Rohrer, D., Taylor, K., & Sholar, B. (2010). Tests enhance the transfer of learning. *Journal of Experimental Psychology: Learning, Memory, and Cognition, 36*, 233–239.
Rudner, L. M., & Boston, C. (1994). Performance assessment. *ERIC Review, 3*(1), 2–12.
Simonson, M., Smaldino, S, Albright, M., & Zvacek, S. (2000). *Teaching and learning at a distance: Foundations of distance education.* Upper Saddle River, NJ: Prentice Hall.
Urtel, M. G., Bahamonde, R. E., Mikesky, A. E., & Vessely, J. S. (2006). On-line quizzing and its effect on student engagement and academic performance. *Journal of Scholarship of Teaching and Learning, 6*(2), 84–92.
White, R. J., & Hammer, C. A. (2000). Quiz-o-Matic: A free Web-based tool for construction of self-scoring on-line quizzes. *Behavior Research Methods, Instruments, & Computers, 32*, 250–253.
Wiggins, G. (1989). A true test: Toward more authentic and equitable assessment. *Phi Delta Kappan, 70*(9), 703–713.
Wilder, D. A., Flood, W. A., & Stromsnes, W. (2001). The use of random extra credit quizzes to increase student attendance. *Journal of Instructional Psychology, 28*, 117–120.
Wiley Education Services. (2018). Retrieved May 1, 2018, from https://edservices.wiley.com

Index

G

I

K

L

M

O

P

Q

S

T

Printed by Libri Plureos GmbH in Hamburg,
Germany

9 781516 526277